MANTRAS AND MUDRAS

This book is written with the motivation of sharing beautiful mantras and mudras with as many people as possible that they may experience the matchless bliss of spiritual awakening … and is dedicated to the long life of my most precious and dearest kind lama, Kyabje Lama Zopa Rinpoche. I also gratefully acknowledge the support of the FPMT (Federation for the Preservation of the Mahayana Tradition), and in particular the venerable Connie Miller, who has assisted with the checking of the precious mantras included in this book. All royalties from this book will be donated to special Buddhist charities.

My lama's teachings are vast and profound
When an ordinary person like me
reflects, thinks, meditates, and communicates,
there is always some error in understanding.
Learned scholars,
If you find my words err
and my meanings mislead,
Please be compassionate and set me right.
Only Buddha is completely without error,
like the sun, the sky's radiant jewel,
dispelling the darkness of night.
LILLIAN TOO

Mantras
and Mudras

Meditations for the hands and voice to bring peace and inner calm

LILLIAN TOO

Element

An imprint of HarperCollins*Publishers*
77-85 Fulham Palace Road
Hammersmith, London W6 8JB

First published in Great Britain in 2002 by Element

10 9 8 7 6 5 4 3 2 1

Printed and bound in Italy by
Editoriale Johnson SpA.

Illustrations by Andy Weber

A catalogue record for this book
is available from the British Library

ISBN 0 00 712 9602

Publisher's Note
Please note that the diagrams for all the hand mudras in this book refer literally to the
positioning of the left and right hand, so the reader should not follow the diagrams as
mirror-images. Reverse the positions of the hands as shown to replicate the mudras.

Contents

PART THREE: MANTRA PRACTICE AND SPECIAL MANTRAS 107

Happiness and suffering
Are dependent
upon your own mind,
upon your interpretation.
They do not come from outside,
from others.
All of your happiness and
all of your suffering
are created by you,
your own mind.

KYABJE LAMA ZOPA RINPOCHE

Introduction

When we recite special mantras, or prayers, and use hand mudras (gestures) to aid our concentration, we are engaging our body, speech, and mind with the motivation of transforming our mind to develop our Buddha potential. Mantras are chanted repeatedly, because transforming the mind takes time; it is a gradual process. Practiced regularly and with sincere motivation, mantras are powerful catalysts for effecting mind transformation, which opens up wonderful pathways to gaining blessings and realizations.

Reciting mantras is not the mere vocal repetition of speech syllables. Meditators know from experience that chanting mantras transcends external sounds and words. It is like listening to a subtle, inner sound that has been inside us since beginningless time.

When you receive a mantra, transmitted by a qualified teacher, the integration of that mantra's wisdom into your consciousness is greatly facilitated. The wisdom-power of mantras enables you to communicate more easily with your own true, inner wisdom, even as you remain detached from external distractions. These distractions impede concentration, thereby creating obstacles. When you recite mantras this agitation of the mind subsides, leaving the mind more at peace. So mantras bring out a special kind of concentration that is strong and integrated. This is known as "single-pointed" concentration.

The mantras you chant should come directly from highly realized beings, from enlightened Masters, and from the Buddha himself. Many of the most powerful Buddhist mantras continue to be chanted in their original Sanskrit, the language of the Buddha, simply because they sound so beautiful and inspiring, and contain such stunning empowerments. But mantras chanted in any language have the same power when recited with strong concentration and sincere motivation.

My teacher Rinpoche once told me this story. A monk visited
a hermit, who lived alone on an island doing retreat. The hermit
had given himself three years to complete chanting ten million
of the powerful six-syllable mantra of the Compassionate
Buddha. The hermit had been told that attaining this
level of practice would awaken his yogic powers.
The mantra was OM MANI PADME HUM.

The monk listened as the hermit did his mantra and, with the
best intention in the world, leaned over to him and whispered,
"I think you have got the pronunciation wrong. This mantra should
be chanted this way ..." and he proceeded to demonstrate. The hermit
listened attentively and then watched as the monk walked back to
his boat to leave the island. Ten minutes later, when the boat was
halfway across the river, the monk heard his name being called and,
looking around, he spied the hermit and heard him call, "Listen to this,
have I got it right now?" and the hermit proceeded to chant the same
mantra, but with the monk's intonation. Astounded, the monk turned
around and saw the hermit walking on the water next to the boat. In
that instant, he realized that the hermit's faith and sincerity had
given his mantra recitation far more power than he had realized.
Getting the intonation correct seemed almost irrelevant.

The mantras selected for inclusion in this book are intended to act as wonderful aids to living and life. These mantras have incredible power to awaken us to the spiritual path in different ways. I learned many of these mantras from my most precious guru, Kyabje Lama Zopa Rinpoche, who also gave me permission to write this book and to include them here.

I have a truly kind, humble and most perfect teacher in Kyabje Lama Zopa Rinpoche, and I have strived diligently to present the mantras, and their explanations, as accurately as possible for the benefit of as many people as possible.

I must stress again and again, however, that any, and all mistakes, misrepresentations, or inadequate explanations of these precious mantras are entirely and completely due to my own imperfect skills.

If reciting these mantras awakens your inner hunger to know more, I strongly urge you to seek out a perfectly qualified teacher. It will simply be the most magnificent thing you will have done in your life.

Personally, the most life-transforming thing that ever happened to me was when I discovered there are Buddhas and Bodhisattvas living among us. They come into the world wearing different disguises. Most of the time they manifest as highly realized Masters who enter our lives and transform it forever. In today's modern world, there are Masters who speak our language and communicate with us like they have known us for a thousand years. They devote their whole existence to passing on the wonderful teachings of the Buddha, and because they are themselves emanations of the Enlightened One, they glow with a radiance of purity that is totally irresistible.

These holy lamas are extremely humble and are extraordinarily kind. They are also highly skilled in leading us to fields of bliss, explaining the meanings of mantras, prayers, and practices. More importantly, these Masters have the power and lineages to grant refuge and give precious initiations that will empower your practice of mantra recitation a million times over. The transmission of mantras, prayers, and practices from such holy beings is what will bring you mountains of blessings, light up paths to new learning, and eventually reveal to you the true nature of reality. It is good karma indeed to meet just such a living Buddha. Chant your mantras and dedicate them sincerely to having such a meeting, and then watch events unfold in your life.

I make two heartfelt dedications.

Firstly, may anyone who sees, touches, reads, remembers, or recites any of the mantras in this book meet perfectly qualified spiritual masters, develop the bodhichitta heart, and immediately attain the strong wish to seek Enlightenment for the sake of all living beings. Secondly, by the merit thus created may my most precious guru, Kyabje Lama Zopa Rinpoche, whose life is so precious to his many thousands of students worldwide, live a long and stable life. May all his holy wishes be fulfilled and actualized immediately, including the building of the Buddha Maitreya statue in Bodhgaya, India.

With love and many mantra prayers,

Lillian Too, June 2001

*The mantra functions in many ways. The reciting of a mantra
a given number of times, combined with concentration, opens
our mind instinctively to supernormal powers and insights.
Mantras can be also be used as therapy for the sick, and can
bring peace to the mentally disturbed. This has been
the experience of many meditators.*

LAMA THUBTEN YESHE

1

first
Steps

Taking refuge mantras

This is the first step on the Buddhist path to inner freedom. It is not anything new. Most of us take refuge already, but in external things. We seek security in money, food, marriage, and even drugs, hoping to find happiness and satisfaction. In the end we realize that all of this is temporary and short term – taking refuge in material pleasures is transient and cannot last.

In a Buddhist sense, taking refuge means turning inward to discover your own mind and your unlimited potential to realize the peerless happiness of a permanent kind – that which comes from giving voice and liberation to your inherent "inner wisdom" energy. The way to realize this inner-mind liberation is to take refuge in the Buddha, Dharma, and Sangha, also known as the "Guru-Triple Gem."

Buddha Refuge means accepting the guidance of enlightened beings as the only solution to the continuing cycle of temporary happiness and suffering.

Dharma Refuge is the wisdom that understands our own true nature. So it means using our inner wisdom immediately, now! Dharma means understanding the true nature of reality.

Sangha Refuge means seeking security in the company of those endowed with wisdom, such as ordained monks and nuns, and also spiritual friends who inspire and support us in our quest for the flowering of our inner-mind wisdom.

This is the mantra of taking refuge in the Guru, the Buddha, the Dharma, and the Sangha:

NAMO GURU BHYE
NAMO BUDDHAYA
NAMO DHARMAYA
NAMO SANGHAYAH

Saying this refuge mantra seven times each morning when you wake up, and seven times at night before you sleep, brings you under the care of the Buddhas; if you have a guru, it brings you under the care of the guru. This simple mantra is extremely powerful because it plants the imprint of taking refuge in the Guru-Triple Gem.

HOMAGE MANTRA TO THE BUDDHA

You can say this longer homage mantra to the Buddha, and incorporate a simple "receiving blessing" visualization. Chant this mantra three times each morning:

LAMA TON PA CHOM DEN DAY
DE ZHIN SHEG PA DRA CHOM PA
YANG DAG PAR DZOG PAY SANG GYAY
PEL GYEL WA, SHAKYA TUB PA LA
CHAG TSEL ZHING, KYAB SU CHI WO
CHO DO JIN GYI LAB TU SOL

TRANSLATION:

To the founder, the endowed transcendent destroyer, the one gone beyond, the foe destroyer, the completely perfect, fully awakened being, the subduer from the Shakya clan, I prostrate. Please grant me your blessings.

As you chant this mantra, feel the presence of the Buddha and take refuge in him. Visualize his body as golden light. He is seated in the Vajra position; his face is very beautiful, and his gaze is compassionate. Rays of light emanate from each pore of the Buddha's body and reach every corner of the world. Feel the rays waft completely over you, entering the top of your head and filling your whole body. Feel very blessed.

Shakyamuni Buddha,
or historical Buddha.

  *mantras and mudras*

Making prostrations

One of the first things that Rinpoche taught me when I met him in Bodhgaya, India, was how beneficial it was to learn how to make prostrations to the holy objects, and especially to images of Buddha. Rinpoche said, "The merit is greater than all the grains of sand on the bed of the river Ganga …"

Rinpoche explained that because most of us have minds that are not purified of karmic obstacles, even if numberless Buddhas were to come in front of us, we would not be able to "see" the aspect of the Buddha, or that which is the pure aspect. We can only see the image of the Buddha shown as in a painting, or as a statue. So when we prostrate to an image of Buddha, in our minds and our hearts we are prostrating to Buddha. The image helps us to visualize. Those of us who have the good karma to meet a perfectly qualified guru can see Buddha emanating as an ordinary being who appears in the form of a humble monk and teacher. This explains why Tibetan Buddhists see His Holiness the Dalai Lama as the Buddha of Compassion. Although he takes the form of an ordinary human being, those who revere him see him as an emanation of the Buddha Chenrezig, the Compassionate Buddha (see page 34). So making prostrations to images of the Buddhas (or holy objects) and to our precious gurus is an act of reverence that precedes all prayers. Making prostrations helps the mind to develop genuine humility, and is a perfect way of overcoming arrogance and pride.

PROSTRATION MANTRA

Prostrate three times while reciting the mantra below. This multiplies it one thousand times. Prostrations purify the negative karma of the body. Verbally reciting mantras exalts the

Buddha, purifying the negative karma of speech. The mental action of remembering the supreme power of the Buddha purifies the negative karma of the mind, thereby arousing faith.

OM NAMO MANJUSHRIYE
NAMA SUSHRIYE
NAMA UTTAMA SHRIYE SVAHA

PROSTRATION MUDRA

If for some reason you find it difficult to make the full-length or even the short prostrations (see opposite), you can visualize yourself prostrating while reciting the mantra. Use your hands to make the Prostration mudra. This mudra is almost universally accepted as the Prayer mudra, symbolizing reverence and respect. Fold your palms together upright, leaving some space in between. Bend the two thumbs inward to signify that the space between the palms is filled with offerings. This makes the mudra more auspicious.

The Prayer mudra, or Namaskara mudra.
This is also the Prostration mudra.

Whether a life situation is wonderful or not depends on the way your mind perceives and interprets it. You can choose to label an experience "wonderful" or "a problem." It depends completely upon your mind, upon your interpretation.

KYABJE LAMA ZOPA RINPOCHE

HOW TO MAKE PROSTRATIONS

There is a short prostration and a full-length prostration. Here is how to practice each one.

First, calm your mind and generate devotional thoughts. Think, "Reverently I prostrate with my body, speech, and mind, and take refuge in the Guru-Triple Gem – Buddha, Dharma, and Sangha." Next, place your palms together, touching the top of your head; then bring them down to touch your forehead; then down again to touch your throat; and then touch your heart (see a, b, c, and d on page 8). Then bend down. Kneel on the floor and place your hands, palms down, on the floor (see e). If you are making the short prostration, lower your forehead until it touches the ground, and then get up. Repeat three times.

For the long prostration, stretch yourself full length on the floor after you have lowered yourself (see f). Raise your palms above your head (see g) and then get up (see h). Do not stay too long on the floor, and make your prostrations with focused concentration. Think reverential thoughts and dedicate the merit created to your own spiritual awakening. Keep your feet together and your fingers closed as you prostrate. The merit gained is simply enormous. As Rinpoche would say, " the merit is like sky!"

a

b

c

d

e

f

g

h

Generating motivation

The sun of real happiness shines
in your life when you start to
cherish others.

KYABJE LAMA ZOPA RINPOCHE

The chanting of mantras becomes extremely powerful when it is practiced with the pure motivation of helping or benefiting others. This altruistic intention develops what Buddhists refer to as "bodhichitta," or the spontaneous kind heart. When you chant this mantra three times to generate powerful motivation before any kind act or prayers, the mantra becomes very meaningful:

DAG DANG ZHEN DON DRUP LAY DU
DAG GI JANG CHUB SEM KYAY DO

TRANSLATION:
To accomplish my own and others' aims
I generate the mind seeking Enlightenment.

Alternatively, you can meditate on the Four Immeasurable Thoughts – your heartfelt wishes for all beings:

Immeasurable equanimity
  May all beings abide in equanimity, free of hatred, anger, and attachment

Immeasurable compassion
  May all beings be free of sufferings and the causes of suffering

Immeasurable love
  May all beings have happiness and the causes of happiness

Immeasurable joy
  May all beings never lose the joys of high rebirth

And may I cause all of these things to happen.

The meditation on the Four Immeasurable Thoughts is considered to be a classic in masterful motivations. Meditate on it.

This is the image of the Dharmachakra, which signifies the teachings of the Buddha. It is placed at the top of Mandala Offerings and is most auspicious.

OVERCOMING ANGER

Anger obscures your mind and makes your everyday life unhappy. Anger causes you and others great problems from day to day. Anger is extremely harmful.

The antidote to anger is patience; as soon as anger begins to arise, you should immediately recognize it and remember its shortcomings. Practice patience and at once there is tranquillity, relaxation, and happiness.

The pain of anger is like red-hot coals in your heart. Anger transforms even a beautiful person into someone ugly and terrifying. What was happy, peaceful, and beautiful completely changes and becomes dark, ugly, and terrifying. As soon as you apply patience, however, anger stops, and as soon as it stops, even your appearance suddenly changes …

KYABJE LAMA ZOPA RINPOCHE

Making mandala offerings

The mandala is a representation of the universe, in its conventional form or as a completely purified realm of existence. There are many different mandalas with distinct concepts and for different purposes. Cosmic mandalas represent our universe and its development; deity mandalas represent our universe as an Enlightened Being's pure realm. In Tibetan Buddhism, deity mandalas are visualized in meditation. They are also painted or created from colored sand as three-dimensional representations for special pujas (ritual offering ceremonies) or initiations; those made of sand are dismantled and dispersed after completion to signify the impermanence of all phenomena.

The mandala offering is one of the most engaging and uplifting of Tibetan Buddhist rituals. During pujas, or to precede teachings and practices, one makes a mandala offering. This is a powerful symbolic prayer offering of the entire universe to all the Buddhas of the ten directions. A mandala offering can be performed either long or short. Also, one can offer a mandala either using a mandala offering set, comprised of a base, rings, and substances that are piled up like a mountain, or with the mandala hand mudra. The mantra that goes with the ritual can either be long or short, depending on which ritual you wish to perform.

Practice making this mandala offering mudra. Place your hands in this mudra in front of you as you recite the mandala offering mantras (either long or short). The two upright fingers in the center signify Mount Meru (the Buddhist axis of the cosmos), while the four corners signify the four continents.

THE SHORT MANDALA OFFERING

SA ZHI PO KYI JUG SHING MAY TOG TRAM
RI RAB LING ZHI NYI DAY GYAN PA DI
SANG GYAY, ZHING DU MIG TAY UL WAR GYI
DRO KUN NAM DAG ZHING LA CHO PAR SHOG

TRANSLATION:

This ground anointed with perfume, and strewn with flowers. In the center is Mount
Meru, around it the four continents, the sun and the moon. I imagine this as a Buddha
Pure Land of bliss and I offer it. May all beings enjoy this Pure Land.

DAG GI CHAG DANG MONG SUM KYAY WAY YUL,
DRA NYEN BAR SUM LU DANG LONG CHO CHAY
PANG PA MAY PAR BUL GYI LEG ZHAY NAY
DUG SUM RANG SAR DROL WAR JIN GYI LOB

TRANSLATION:

The objects of attachment, aversion, and ignorance – my friends, my enemies,
and strangers. My body, my wealth, and my enjoyments. I offer these with no sense
of loss. Please accept them with pleasure and bless me with freedom from the three
poisons of anger, attachment, and ignorance.

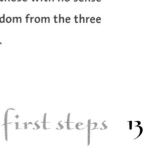

THE LONG MANDALA OFFERING

To perform this very auspicious and powerful ritual you need the mandala offering set, which comprises a base and three rings. Mandala sets can be purchased in India, Nepal, Tibet, and most Buddhist meditation centers around the world. They are usually made of silver and plated with gold. The belief is that the more valuable your mandala offering base, the more auspicious the effects of the ritual. For the filling, you can use rice, wheat, or other grains, and you can place as many precious things as you wish with the grain. I use a mixture of semi-precious stones – crystal, amethyst, tiger's eye, jade, citrine, quartz, lapis lazuli, malachite, amber, coral, and so forth. To add greater value to my offering, I also include a few precious stones. You should use beads and colored stones, or anything that symbolizes something of value to you. Always keep your mandala set wrapped up in soft velvet or silk when you are not using it.

The Method

Take some grain in your left hand and hold the mandala base. With your right hand, sprinkle some grain on the base. Wipe the base clockwise three times with your right forearm, tipping the grain away from you. Visualize purifying incorrect motivation. Put more grain on the base. Wipe anti-clockwise three times with your right forearm, tipping the grain toward yourself. Visualize receiving great blessings from the merit field (the buddhas, gurus, or both, whose visualization bestows merit) to offer the mandala from your heart. Spread more grain to symbolize precious jewels.

The Long Mandala Mantra (English translation)

Recite the following:

🔔 *OM vajra ground AH HUM, the mighty golden ground.*

Place the first ring on the base.

🔔 *OM vajra fence AH HUM, the iron fence around the edge. In the center is Mount Meru.*
In the east the continent Lupapo (Tall-Body Land). In the south, Dzambuling
(Rose-Apple Land).
In the west, Balangcho (Cattle-Gift Land). In the north, Draminyan.
In the east, the sub-continents Lu and Lupag, in the south, Ngayab and Ngayabzhan.
In the west, Yodan and Lamchog dro, in the north, Draminyan and Draminyan Gyida.
Here's the precious mountain; the wish-granting tree; the wish-fulfilling cow; the
unploughed harvest.

Place the second ring on the base. Visualize placing Eight Precious Objects belonging to a
wheel-turning king who rules the four continents.

🔔 *The precious wheel; the precious jewel; the precious queen; the precious minister; the*
precious elephant; the precious horse; the precious general; the great treasure vase.

Continue on the inner area of the second ring. Say the following:

🔔 *The goddess of grace; the goddess of garlands; the goddess of songs; the goddess of*
dance; the goddess of flowers; the goddess of incense; the goddess of light; the goddess
of perfume.

Place the third ring. Say the following:

 The sun, the moon, the precious parasol, the banner of victory in all directions. In the center are the most perfect riches of gods and humans, with nothing missing, pure and delightful.

Place the Dharmachakra (the top object, usually a jewel-encrusted wheel) on top of the built-up mandala.

Making the Offering

To my holy and most kind guru, to all the lineage gurus, to the Buddha and the entire assembly of Buddhas of the ten directions I offer this mandala as a Buddha-field. Please accept this mandala offering with compassion, for the sake of all beings. Having accepted them, please bestow on me and on all beings abiding as far as the limits of space your inspiration with loving compassion. Please bless us with freedom from the three poisons — anger, attachment, and ignorance.

Hold the mandala at the level of your heart and offer it while reciting the mandala Completion mantra:

IDAM GURU RATNA MANDALAKAM NIRYATAYAMI

THE LONG MANDALA MANTRA

OM VAJRA BHUMI AH HUM, WANG CHEN SER GYI SA ZHI
OM VAJRA REKHE AH HUM; CHI CHAG RI-KOR YUG-GYI
KOR-WAY U-SU; RIGYEL PO-RI RAB

SHAR LU PAG-PO; LHO DZAM BU-LING
NUB BA LANG-CHO; JANG DRA MI NYEN

LU DANG LU-PAG; NGA YAB DANG, NGA YAB ZHEN
YO DEN DANG-LAM CHOG-DRO
DRA-MI NYEN-DANG; DRA-MI NYEN GYI-DA
RINPOCHAY RI-WO; PAG SAM GYI SHING
DOJO BA MA MO PA-YI LO-TOG

KOR LO RINPOCHAY, NORBU RINPOCHAY
TZUN MO RINPOCHAY; LON PO RINPOCHAY
LANGPO RINPOCHAY, TA CHOG RINPOCHAY
MAG PON RINPOCHAY, TER CHEN PO-YI BUM-PA

GEG-MA TRENG WA-MA, LU-MA
GAR-MA, ME-TOG-MA, DUG PO-MA
NANG SEL-MA, DRI CHAB-MA
NYI-MA DA-WA RINPOCHE DUG
CHOG-LAY NAM-PAR, GYEL WAY GYEL-TSEN
U-SU LHA DANG MI

PEL JOR PUN-SUM TSOG-PA; MA-TSANG WAMAY-PA
TSANG ZHING YID DU, WONG-WA

DI DAG DRIN-CHEN TSA WA, DANG GYU PAR
CHAY PAY PEL DEN; LAMA DAM-PA NAM DANG
KYAY PER DU YANG
LAMA LOSANG TUB-WANG DORJE CHANG

CHEN-PO LHA-TSOG KOR-DANG CHAY-PAY NAM-LA ZHING
KAM UL WAR GYIO
TUG JAY DRO-WAY DON-DU ZHAY SU SOL
ZHAY NAY KYANG DAG-SOG DRO-WA
MAR-GYUR; NAM KAY TA DANG-NYAM PAY
SEM CHEN-TAM CHAY-LA
TUG TSE WA CHEN PO GO NAY JIN GYI LAB TU SOL

RINPOCHE'S ADVICE ON THE IMMENSE SPIRITUAL BENEFITS OF MAKING THE MANDALA OFFERING

" [The] mandala offering is an extremely powerful method for accumulating extensive merits and receiving realizations such as bodhichitta and emptiness quickly. Just as great strength is needed to carry a heavy load, a great amount of merit is needed to lead all sentient beings to Enlightenment. There is nothing

that can be offered with your hands that is more meritorious
than offering mandalas.

"The mandala offering contains the practice of all six perfections. The six
Buddhist perfections are: generosity, morality, patience, joyous effort,
meditative concentration, and wisdom.

"By cleaning and blessing the mandala base with a special liquid, you practice
the perfection of generosity. Checking the grain for insects results in the perfection of moral conduct, and removing insects from the grain without harming
them leads to the perfection of patience. By thinking of how fortunate you are
to be able to practice Dharma and making the offering with joy, you cultivate
joyous effort. By not forgetting the visualization, you attain concentration. By
clearly visualizing the colors and objects in the mandala, wisdom is attained.
Therefore, offering mandalas helps you to quickly complete the two
accumulations of the merits of method and wisdom, as it contains
all the six perfections.

"This practice pacifies all hindrances to your temporal and ultimate happiness.
These depend on merit, and merit depends on offerings. The most meritorious
object to offer is the mandala. Therefore if you wish to achieve temporal and
ultimate happiness, you can make many mandala offerings.

"Lama Tsong Khapa (a fifteenth-century lama who founded the Gelugpa tradition of Tibetan Buddhism) offered 1,800,000 mandala offerings and achieved
all the realizations of the stages and paths. If you wish to gain realizations you
should offer mandala offerings to your guru every day, to his jewel-like body,

and so bestow the sphere of great bliss in an instant. All realizations
depend on your guru.

"Offering mandalas to your guru is like offering gifts to a king before
requesting a favor of him. Achieving Enlightenment in one lifetime depends on
your relationship with your guru."

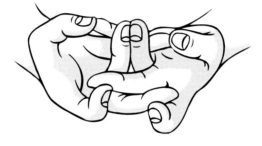

mantras and mudras

Purifying the space and ground

An important part of the preliminary ritual to reciting mantras and practicing meditation is to ensure that the space and ground where one does one's practice is kept clean and pure. There are mantras for cleaning, and visualizations for purifying the place of meditation.

A CLEANSING MEDITATION

When you clean with a cloth or broom, think "This is to sweep away all the defilements, negative thoughts, and obstacles that block my true awakening." Recite the following two-word mantra at least 108 times each day:

DURUPANG, TIMAPANG

As you dust and remove stains in the room, think of your anger, attachment, and ignorance being erased, disappearing. Stains are subtle defilements that cause blocks in your life; wipe them away daily.

This is a powerful mantra. Recite this mantra daily as you sweep and clean, and visualize all the dust and dirt entering the ground.

A PURIFICATION VISUALIZATION

Imagine an unimaginably large place where the ground is smooth, flat, and made of gold. There are exquisite designs of lapis lazuli on the gold, like you sometimes see in beautiful thangkas (paintings on cloth). The ground is very soft, just like a sponge mattress; as you step on it, it sinks down four or five inches (10 to 13 centimeters) then springs up. And whenever you touch this ground, you feel a deep sense of bliss. It is not an empty place; there are many precious and beautiful trees growing there, and perched on those trees are many birds who are transformations of Buddhas, talking about Dharma. There are pools with crystal-clear water for bathing and ponds that have golden, radiating sand on the bottom. Precious mountains made of precious jewels border this vast golden ground.

This is the visualization to use when you say the prayer for purifying space. Do not visualize rocks, thorns, or lots of garbage around. It should be clean and pure, and very beautiful.

Then think:

Everywhere may the ground be pure, free of the roughness of pebbles and stones and so forth. May it be in the nature of lapis lazuli, and as smooth as the palm of a child's hand.

Why is the sky blue?

I am often asked, why is the sky blue? Why is the sky blue

and not red, yellow or some other color? The answer is

related to Mount Meru [the Buddhist axis of the cosmos].

We are in the southern continent of Mount Meru, and the

teachings explain that the sky is blue because of the bright-

ness of the southern side of Mount Meru, which is all lapis

lazuli. This blue sky is also reflected in the water, so this is

why you also see blue oceans in our world.

KYABJE LAMA ZOPA RINPOCHE

Asking for a mountain of blessings

MEDITATING ON THE BUDDHA

On the lotus, sun and moon seat visualize Shakyamuni Buddha, the historical Buddha who has attained perfect realizations and left this world a legacy of perfect teachings. He manifests the omniscient mind of all the Buddhas. He is the ultimate teacher, the guru, and he is therefore inseparable from your own guru. He shows the unmistaken path and is bound by infinite compassion, to you and to all beings.

Buddha's body, in golden light, is magnificent. He wears the three robes of a monk. His face is beautiful. His eyes see all others and you. His gaze is peaceful. His mind is free of all critical thoughts. He accepts you fully.

His right hand touches the earth, signifying control over the maras (enemies of the mind) of desire. His left hand holds a bowl of nectar, symbolizing conquest of samsaric aggregates. (In general, the term "samsaric aggregates" refers to the constituents of body and mind that make up the individual who is still caught in "samsara". That is, a person still under the control and influence of karma and the delusions, specifically the three poisons of attachment, anger and ignorance.) His body is in the Vajra posture, signifying that he has destroyed death and his own four maras. He is surrounded by light beams, signifying that he is compassionately working for all beings.

Shakyamuni Buddha symbolizes all that is compassionate.

He signifies triumph over the maras, or enemies of the mind.

THE BUDDHA'S HOLY MANTRA

Recite one mala or rosary (108 times) as you visualize millions of golden light rays emanating from the Buddha's body and entering your body through the crown of your head. This mantra brings down a shower of blessings, a mountain of blessings . . .

TADYATHA OM MUNI MUNI MAHA MUNIYE SVAHA

THE BUDDHA'S HAND MUDRAS AND THEIR MEANINGS

From left: the Teaching mudra, the Protection mudra, and the Mudra of fearlessness.

Making dedications

After every meditation, prayer session, or good deed, it is important to dedicate the positive potential created by your virtuous practices and actions. This serves to "lock in" all the merit created by your transformation exercises, and capture the wonderful moments of positive mind awareness. So each time you chant a mantra, work with a hand mudra, make offerings, or simply meditate on the Buddha's teachings, you are creating merit. Do not forget to make a list of dedications after the sessions; otherwise, all the merit earned will get destroyed by a moment of impulsive anger and an instant of holding wrong views. Rinpoche stresses this again and again. After every teaching or food offering, Rinpoche's list of dedications are so long that they seem to go on forever. Yet not a single dedication is ever for his own benefit. All Rinpoche's dedications are for others.

I discovered a stunning secret in the course of following Rinpoche. It is that the most powerful prayers are those that are made to benefit others. When you think of others, your mantras take on awesome power. So always chant your mantras to benefit others; say your prayers to benefit others. This is the source of greatest happiness.

One of the most powerful dedications is to pray for the development of bodhichitta, which is the compassionate heart and mind wishing to attain Enlightenment for the benefit of others.

GAY WA DI YI NYUR DU DAG
LAMA SANG GYAY DRUB GYUR NAY
DRO WA CHIG KYANG MA LU PA
KYE KYI SA LA GO PAR SHOG

JANG CHUB SEM CHOG RIN PO CHE
MA KYAY PA NAM KYAY GYUR CHIG
KYAY PA NYAM PA MAY PA YANG
GONG NAY GONG DU PEL WAR SHOG

TRANSLATION:

Due to this merit may I soon attain the enlightened state of buddhahood, that I may liberate all sentient beings from their sufferings. May the precious bodhichitta mind in me, not yet born, arise and grow. May that born have no decline but increase forever more.

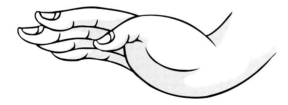

The mudra of bodhichitta, or compassion.

One of my favorite dedications

Due to the positive potential I have created with

my meditative practice today, may anyone who

merely sees, hears, remembers, touches, or talks

about the Feng Shui in any of my books be freed in

that very instant from all their sufferings, and may

they abide in happiness forever. May all their

problems be solved immediately and may each

person find peace and happiness.

2

The
Mantras

The most famous mantra in the world

OM MANI PADME HUM

Those endowed with a skillful wisdom will naturally attain realizations through the power of mantra. Practitioners of mantra yoga will discover that their inner sound becomes completely one with the mantra itself. Then even their normal speech becomes mantra.

This six-syllable mantra is the most famous mantra in the world. Many Buddhist practitioners chant it daily; many Tibetan Buddhists chant this mantra continually all through their lives. This wonderfully powerful mantra is the mantra of the much-loved Buddha of Compassion, known as the Buddha Chenrezig in Tibet, as the Goddess of Mercy, Kuan Yin, by Chinese all over the world, as Avalokiteshvara in India, and as the Goddess Kwannon in Japan. If you chant only one mantra in your life, let it be this one.

It is said that reciting this mantra 100,000 times will awaken hidden yogic abilities within you. This mantra has the power to calm your fears, soothe your worries, and answer all your prayers. This is the mantra that is rolled and kept inside prayer wheels, printed on prayer flags, and written on stones known as Mani stones. Placed in the path of moving water, the mantra purifies the water so that all the animals and insects that drink the water are instantly purified. Those printed on prayer flags bless the winds that blow, thereby spreading blessings to all who are touched by the wind.

One of the best commitments to make to oneself is to create a goal to chant one million OM MANI PADME HUMs. Give yourself a year to do it, and then watch as your mind starts to develop awareness, insights, and deep feelings of compassion. The power of this simple mantra is truly amazing.

I chanted this mantra in the latter years of my corporate hey days in Hong Kong, and soon after I had completed a great many of these mantras I met my precious guru. I know that the mantra brought Rinpoche into my life – and now, having met Rinpoche I shudder to think what my life would have been like if I had not met him.

THE MEDITATION AND RECITATION OF THE GREAT COMPASSIONATE ONE: FOUR-ARMED CHENREZIG

*Chenrezig, the Buddha of Compassion, is the equivalent to the
goddess Kwannon in Japan, and the Chinese deity Kuan Yin.*

Gaze at the image of four-armed Chenrezig so you make a lasting imprint in your mind. Take note of the symbols she carries in her four hands. Think of Chenrezig seated on the moon disk on a lotus, on top of your head. Then make a strong prayer, reciting the following mantra:

 *I pray to you, my guru, Chenrezig. I pray to you, perfect noble one, Chenrezig. I pray to you, lord protector, Chenrezig. I pray to you, lord of love, Chenrezig.*

Buddha of great compassion, hold me fast in your compassion. From time without beginning, beings have wandered in samsara, undergoing unendurable suffering. They have no other protector than you. Please bless them that they may achieve the omniscient state of the Buddha.

Om mani padme hum

Sentient beings through the force of anger, now born in the hell realms, experience the suffering of painful heat and cold. May they all be reborn in your perfect Pure Land.

Om mani padme hum

Sentient beings, through the force of greed, are born in the hungry spirit realm and experience the sufferings of hunger and thirst. May they all be reborn in your perfect pure realm.

Om mani padme hum

Sentient beings, through the force of ignorance now born as animals, experience the suffering of dullness and stupidity. May they be reborn in your presence.

Om mani padme hum

Sentient beings, through the force of nonvirtue, are born as human beings, experiencing the sufferings of birth, sickness, old age, and death. May they be reborn in your pure realm.

Om mani padme hum

Sentient beings, through the force of jealousy, are born among demigods and experience the suffering of fighting and quarreling. May they be reborn in your realm, the Potala.

Om mani padme hum

Sentient beings, through the force of pride, are born in the realm of gods and experience the suffering of change and falling. May they be born in your realm, the Potala.

Om mani padme hum

May I, myself, through all my existences, act in the same manner as Chenrezig. This means may all beings be liberated from the impure realms, and may the most perfect sound of the six-syllable mantra spread in the ten directions.

By the power of this prayer to you, most noble and perfect one, may all beings take karma and its effects into account, and practice skillful means diligently. May they meet fully qualified perfect spiritual masters and take up the practice of Dharma for the good of all.

Meditate like this as you recite the mantra OM MANI PADME HUM.

Recite the mantra as many times as you can. Finally, let the mind remain absorbed in its own essence, without making distinctions between subject, object, and act.

Do not forget to make your dedication.

THE LONG MANTRA OF THOUSAND-ARMED CHENREZIG

Gaze at the image of thousand-armed Chenrezig. The thousand arms symbolize Chenrezig ever-ready to attend to all the suffering beings of the world. Let the image of Chenrezig remain in your mind forever.

Recite one mala (108 chants) of OM MANI PADME HUM, and generate a pure motivation that you are chanting these mantras to benefit all beings and especially your loved ones. Then recite the powerful long mantra of the thousand-armed Chenrezig:

O Arya, compassionate-eyed one, you who are the treasure of compassion, I request you, please listen to me. Please guide myself, and all mothers and fathers, in all six realms to be freed quickly from the great ocean of samsara. I request that the vast and profound peerless-awakening mind may grow. With the tear of your great compassion, please cleanse all karma and delusion. Please lead with your hand of compassion, migrators and me to fields of bliss. Please Amitabha and Chenrezig, in all my lives be virtuous friends. Show well the undeceptive pure path, and quickly place us in Buddha's state.

THE LONG MANTRA OF THE COMPASSIONATE BUDDHA
RECITE AT LEAST THREE TIMES

NAMO RATNA TRA YA YA/NAMA ARYA JÑANA SAGARA
VAIROCHANA BYUHA RAJAYA/TATHAGATAYA
NAMA SARVA TATHAGATE BHYA/ARHATE BHYA SAMYAKSAM
BUDDHE BHYA/NAMA ARYA
AVALOKITESHVARA/BODHISATVAYA/MAHA SATTVAYA
MAHA KARUNI KAYA/TADYATHA/OM DHARA DHARA/DHIRI
DHIRI DHURU DHURU/ITTE VATTE CHALE CHALE/PRACHALE
PRACHALE KUSUME KUSUME VARE/ILI MILI/CHITI JALA
APANAYE SVAHA

DEDICATIONS

Due to this merit may I soon attain the enlightened state of Chenrezig that I may be able to liberate all sentient beings from their sufferings. May the precious compassionate mind in me not yet born now arise and grow. May that which has arisen never decline, but increase forever more.

By the force of these praises and requests made to you, may all disease, poverty, wars, intolerance, fighting, and quarrels in the world be pacified. May the wish for Dharma and all auspiciousness increase throughout the countries of the world, and in all directions where all others and I dwell.

mantras and mudras

Eight-armed Chenrezig, the Compassionate Buddha.

A representation of Om mani padme hum. Each segment of the circle contains one syllable of the mantra.

the mantras **39**

MEDITATION ON THE EIGHT VERSES OF THOUGHT TRANSFORMATION

These verses might seem severe if you are meeting them for the first time, but they are excellent for subduing the angry reactive mind. These verses help us practice taking an extreme posture and attitude of humility, which is not easy. This is why we need the help of the Compassionate Buddha. And then when we do succeed in transforming our minds, we will realize how easy (as well as satisfying and fulfilling) it is to take these humble attitudes. After each verse, visualize much light coming from Chenrezig flowing into you and completely filling your whole body. It purifies selfishness and ignorance, which prevent you from understanding the meaning of a particular verse. It gives you the ability to understand and integrate each verse as fully as possible into your daily life.

Say one mala (108 chants) of the six-syllable mantra while doing this meditation:

Om mani padme hum

1   *With the determination to obtain the greatest possible benefit from all sentient beings, who are more precious than a wish-fulfilling jewel, and to attain Enlightenment solely for their benefit, I shall hold them most dear at all times.*

Om mani padme hum

2   *Whenever I am with others, I will always see myself as the lowest of all. And from the very depth of my heart, I will respectfully hold others as supreme.*

Om mani padme hum

3   In all actions, I will examine my mind and the moment a disturbing attitude arises, endangering myself and others, I will firmly confront and avert it.

Om mani padme hum

4   Whenever I meet a person of bad nature who is overwhelmed by negative actions and intense suffering, I will hold such a rare one dear, as if I had found a precious treasure.

Om mani padme hum

5   When others, out of jealousy, mistreat me with abuse, slander and so on, I will accept defeat and offer the victory to them.

Om mani padme hum

6   When someone I have benefited and in whom I have placed great trust hurts me very badly, I will practice seeing that person as my supreme teacher.

Om mani padme hum

7   In short, I will offer directly and indirectly every benefit and happiness to all beings, my mothers. I will practice in secret taking upon myself all their harmful actions and sufferings.

Om mani padme hum

8   Without these practices being defiled by the stains of the eight worldly concerns and perceiving without grasping all phenomena as illusory, I will release all beings from the bondage of the disturbing, unsubdued mind and karma.

Mantras for purifying negative karma

The karma of the sentient mind never just fades away, even in hundreds of millions of years. When the causes convene and the time is come, the consequences can do nothing but flower.

WORDS SPOKEN BY LORD BUDDHA HIMSELF

The way karma works is beyond comprehension. Only the All-Knowing know it.

SHANTIDEVA

As you sow, so shall you reap.

ANON

When you think about all the obstacles in your life, all the things that constantly go wrong, all the sadness and grief that befall humankind, again and again, it really makes you think about karma, negative karma. To Buddhists of all lineages, karma is the central core around which they build their practice of ultimate kindness and compassion.

So consider this reflective meditation. Think about it deeply, and with concentration.

The negative karma we have accumulated from beginning-less time is as extensive as the ocean. I know this leads to eons of suffering, yet I constantly create negative karma. I try to avoid nonvirtue and practice positive acts, yet day and night without respite, negativity and moral downfalls come to me like rainfall.

I lack the ability to purify these faults and with these negative imprints in my mind, I could suddenly die and fall to an unfortunate rebirth. I could be reborn in the lower realms, as an animal, a hungry ghost. I could get reborn in the hell realms or as a beggar in this realm. I must purify all my negative karma, wash them out and accumulate good karma instead.

There are two very popular Buddhist practices to purify negative karma: the practice of Vajrasattva (see page 44), which involves chanting the purification mantra, and the practice of Confession to the 35 Confession Buddhas (see page 48), which involves the body mudra of prostration.

The double dorje, or double vajra (thunderbolt), a holy implement that is used in Buddhist rituals and practices.

1. THE PRACTICE AND MANTRAS OF BUDDHA VAJRASATTVA

Vajrasattva is the Buddha of Purification. His 100-syllable mantra is the core practice of many Buddhists because the purification practice of Vajrasattva is so powerful. I have obtained permission from my precious teacher to reproduce his mantras, both long and short, in this book. Also included here is the Vajrasattva Meditation, which is so powerful for dissolving blocks and obstacles. Learn the mantras and chant them daily. They are exhilarating and uplifting. Should you ever have the opportunity to receive an oral transmission of the mantras from a fully qualified guru, it will give your mantra purification practice a million times more power!

Start with the visualization of Buddha Vajrasattva (see the illustration on page 47). Visualize Vajrasattva floating above your head, seated on an open white lotus on a moon disc. He is white, translucent, and adorned with beautiful ornaments and clothes. His right hand, holding a Vajra, symbolic of Great bliss, is in the mudra of the Three Jewels at his heart; his left hand, holds a bell, symbolic of the wisdom of emptiness.

The vajra and bell signify his attainment of the enlightened state. At his heart is the seed-syllable HUM and the letters of Vajrasattva's 100-syllable mantra standing clockwise around the edge of the moon disk.

From the HUM at Vajrasattva's heart, light radiates in all directions, requesting the Buddhas to bestow their blessings. They send white rays of light and nectar, which absorb into the HUM and the letters of the mantra at Vajrasattva's heart. They fill his whole body, enhancing the magnificence of his appearance and the brilliance of his mantra. And from his heart white light and nectar flows through your crown chakra (at the crown of the head) and into you, and so completely purifying all the negativities inside you, your speech, your heart, and your mind.

Keep thinking, "Please Vajrasattva, with your great compassion, please purify me from the misery of millions of eons' worth of negative karma accumulated since beginningless times."

THE 100-SYLLABLE VAJRASATTVA MANTRA

(chant this mantra 28 times)

OM VAJRASATTVA SAMAYA
MANU PALAYA
VAJRASATTVA DENO PA TITA
DIDO MAY BHAVA
SUTO KAYO MAY BHAVA
SUPO KAYO MAY BHAVA
ANU RAKTO MAY BHAVA
SARVA SIDDHI MAY PRAYATSA
SARVA KARMA SU TSA MAY
TSITTAM SHRIYAM KURU HUM
HA HA HA HA HO BHAGAVAN
SARVA TATHAGATA VAJRA MA MAY MUN TSA
VAJRA BHAVA MAHA SAMAYA SATTVA AH HUM PEY

The short mantra of Vajrasattva is:

OM VAJRASATTVA HUM

Recite this 108 times.

THE VISUALIZATION OF PURIFICATION

Do these visualizations as you chant the mantra:

The negativities of the body take the form of black ink. Imagine it flushed out by the light and nectar leaving your body like filthy liquid flowing down a drainpipe. Feel they no longer exist.

The negativities of speech take the form of liquid tar. Light and nectar fill your body, making the negativities rise to the top and flow out through the upper openings of your body. Feel they no longer exist.

Your disturbing attitudes and mental negativities appear as darkness in your heart. When struck by the forceful stream of light and nectar, the darkness completely vanishes. It simply ceases to exist. Feel it is completely nonexistent.

Do the three visualizations simultaneously. This sweeps away the subtle obscurations that prevent you from seeing correctly all that exists. Feel completely free of these obscurations.

Visualize your negative speech, actions, and mental obscurations being gently pushed out of your body, and beautiful white light filling you with purity and serenity. A feeling of being completely cleansed overwhelms you.

Doing the Vajrasattva practice is not simply about reciting the mantra and saying some prayers. It is about making the practice effective for your mind, making it the quickest, most powerful way to transform your mind.

KYABJE LAMA ZOPA RINPOCHE

Vajrasattva is the Buddha of Purification. Meditate on him and visualize negativities flowing out of the body.

Completion of the Practice

Make this promise to Vajrasattva, specifying a period of time for which you intend to keep it. The promise is, of course, to yourself. To make it easy for you, promise to keep your thoughts, speech, and actions free of negative karma for just 24 hours. This will make your promise achievable.

"I shall not create these negative actions from now until _____."

Visualize Vajrasattva being extremely pleased and he says to you, "My spiritual child of the essence, all your negativities, obscurations, and degenerated vows have been completely purified."

With delight, Vajrasattva slowly dissolves and then melts into white light before absorbing into you. Your body, speech, and mind become inseparably one with Vajrasattva's holy body, speech, and mind. Concentrate on this.

Finally, do not forget your dedications.

2. PROSTRATIONS TO THE 35 CONFESSION BUDDHAS

Reciting the names of the 35 Confession Buddhas and making prostrations to them is one of the most powerfully purifying of the preliminary practices. I first learned to do this practice at the month-long meditation course I attended in Kopan Monastery in 1997. Kopan sits on top of a hill above the legendary Boudhanath Stupa in Kathmandu, Nepal. The mighty, snowcapped Himalayas rise imposingly behind and in front lays the Kathmandu valley. At dawn each day the clouds nudge at one's feet and the air feels pure and light and blissful. Being in Kopan is like being in Pure Land.

Each morning we would wake at 5am to do this purification practice. In addition to it being wonderful exercise, it gave many of us a stunning feeling of release because it involved our bodies (the act of prostration), our speech (reciting the names of the 35 Confession Buddhas), and our minds (concentrating on our motivation). For those who want to open doors to the pure inner soul – the Buddha essence – within them, this practice is one of the most effective ways of scrubbing away the grime and dirt of negative karma that has collected and imprisoned this inner purity over many lifetimes. Spiritual awakening is blissful only when it reveals the purity within.

Kyabje Lama Zopa Rinpoche once explained to me that:

 "... It says in the teachings that those with strong devotion can purify 80,000 eons of negative karmas by reciting just once the holy name of Guru Shakyamuni Buddha… this is the quick way to do the practice. If you want to do a certain number of prostrations, such as 35, this way of doing it is very good. While you are doing the first prostration, you recite Guru Shakyamuni Buddha's holy name:

TON PA CHOM DEN DAY, DE ZHIN SHEG PA DRA CHOM PA, YANG DAG PA, DZOG PAY SANG GYAY, PEL GYEL WA, SHAKYA TUB PA LA, CHAG TSEL LO

"... and just keep on reciting it until you finish that prostration."

Shakyamuni Buddha

mantras and mudras

RINPOCHE'S ADVICE ON HOW TO DO PROSTRATIONS TO THE 35 BUDDHAS

"Putting your two thumbs inside your palms signifies offering a jewel. You cannot prostrate with empty hands. The two hands signify the path you are going to achieve, with method and wisdom.

"You first put your hands on top of your head, then at the forehead, then at the throat, then at the heart. Prostration at each of these points becomes the cause to achieve the holy signs of the Buddha's holy body, the pinnacle at the top and the central hair at the forehead. Prostrating at the throat creates the karma to achieve the qualities of the Buddha's holy speech, and at the heart, the qualities of the holy mind, the omniscient mind.

"There are two types of prostration: complete, or full prostrations, and five-limb (short) prostrations. The lineage of full-length prostrations came from the great yogi Naropa. Whether you do a full-length or a five-limb prostration, you should touch your head to the ground. You should not do prostrations simply by touching your body and not your head to the floor, thinking it is dirty, because this doesn't become a five-limb prostration. As soon as you touch your head to the ground, you should stand up quickly; you should not lie down for a long time. Getting up quickly from the ground signifies being liberated quickly from samsara.

"When you make prostrations, do not spread your fingers like a duck's foot. Prostrate in a respectful way, keeping your fingers together.

"As you stand up, a replica of Guru Shakyamuni Buddha absorbs into you, and you think that your body, speech, and mind become one with the essence of Guru Shakyamuni Buddha's holy body, holy speech, and holy mind.

"After the replica of Guru Shakyamuni Buddha absorbs into you, think, 'My body, speech, and mind have become the essence of Guru Shakyamuni Buddha's holy body, holy speech, and holy mind. My obscurations and negative karmas are purified.' After thinking this, think that the body, speech, and mind of all your past lives and of all other sentient beings have become one with Guru Shakyamuni Buddha's holy body, holy speech, and holy mind, and that all the negative karmas and obscurations of all other sentient beings have been purified.

"This is the way to visualize when you make prostrations to any Buddha. First you visualize the rays coming and purifying; then second, a replica of the Buddha absorbing into you so that you become one.

"Each time you make a prostration you repeat the name of the Buddha over and over again. After you have finished that prostration, you repeat the second Buddha's name over and over again until you have finished the second prostration. If you do this, when you have finished the 35 prostrations, you have finished repeating the 35 Buddhas' names many times.

"If you are doing only 35 prostrations, at the same time as you finish the 35 prostrations you finish repeating the 35 Buddhas' names, so then you can recite the rest of the prayer. But if you are doing 100 prostrations at a time, after 35 prostrations, without completing the rest of the prayer, you go back and start from Guru Shakyamuni Buddha again, do 35 prostrations, then again go back and do another 35. In this way you do a little more than 100 – 105, in fact – so you can put the extra five in your pocket. You can save it for coffee. After doing 100 prostrations like this, you can then recite the rest of the prayer."

PROSTRATIONS TO THE 35 CONFESSION BUDDHAS – A POWERFUL PURIFICATION PRACTICE

Begin with the Prostration mantra. Make three prostrations while reciting this mantra:

OM NAMO MANJUSHRIYE, NAMA SUSHRIYE,
NAMA UTTAMA SHRIYE SVAHA

Then say:

I (say your name), throughout all time, take refuge in the guru; I take refuge in the Buddhas; I take refuge in the Dharma; I take refuge in the Sangha.

The 35 Buddhas are grouped in five groups, according to the five Buddha families, each with their specific color, with seven Buddhas in each group. The recitation for each is preceded with "To Tathagata," which means "to the one thus gone":

1. To the Founder, Bhagavan, Tathagata, arhat, Perfectly Completed Buddha, Glorious Conqueror Shakyamuni Buddha, I prostrate.

4. To Tathagata King, Lord of the Nagas, I prostrate.

5. To Tathagata Army of Heroes, I prostrate.

2. To Tathagata Thoroughly Destroying with Vajra Essence, I prostrate.

6. To Tathagata Delighted Hero, I prostrate.

3. To Tathagata Radiant Jewel, I prostrate.

7. To Tathagata Jewel Fire, I prostrate.

8. To Tathagata
Jewel Moonlight,
I prostrate.

12. To Tathagata
Bestowed with
Courage, I prostrate.

9. To Tathagata
Meaningful to See,
I prostrate.

13. To Tathagata
Pure One,
I prostrate.

10. To Tathagata
Jewel Moon,
I prostrate.

14. To Tathagata
Bestowed with
Purity, I prostrate.

11. To Tathagata
Stainless One,
I prostrate.

15. To Tathagata
Water God,
I prostrate.

the mantras **55**

16. To Tathagata
Deity of the Water
God, I prostrate.

20. To Tathagata
Glorious Light,
I prostrate.

17. To Tathagata
Glorious Goodness,
I prostrate.

21. To Tathagata
Sorrowless Glory,
I prostrate.

18. To Tathagata
Glorious Sandalwood,
I prostrate.

22. To Tathagata
Son of Noncraving,
I prostrate.

19. To Tathagata
Infinite Splendor,
I prostrate.

23. To Tathagata
Glorious Flower,
I prostrate.

24. To Tathagata
Pure Light Rays
Clearly Knowing
by Play,
I prostrate.

28. To Tathagata
Glorious Name
Widely Renowned,
I prostrate.

25. To Tathagata
Lotus Light Rays
Clearly Knowing
by Play, I prostrate.

29. To Tathagata
King Holding the
Victory Banner of
Foremost Power,
I prostrate.

26. To Tathagata
Glorious Wealth,
I prostrate.

30. To Tathagata
Glorious One Totally
Subduing, I prostrate.

27. To Tathagata
Glorious Mindfulness,
I prostrate.

31. To Tathagata
Utterly Victorious
in Battle, I prostrate.

32. To Tathagata
Glorious
Transcendence
Through Subduing,
I prostrate.

34. To Tathagata
All-Subduing Jewel
Lotus, I prostrate.

33. To Tathagata
Glorious
Manifestations
Illuminating All,
I prostrate.

35. To Tathagata, arhat,
Perfectly Completed
Buddha King of the Lord
of Mountains, Firmly
Seated on Jewel and
Lotus, I prostrate.
(Say three times.)

THE CONFESSION TO THE 35 BUDDHAS

All you thirty-five Buddhas, and those thus gone, foe destroyers, fully enlightened ones
and transcendent destroyers who are existing, sustaining, and living throughout the ten
directions, our worlds.

All you Buddhas, please give me your attention.

In this life, and throughout beginningless lives, in all the realms of samsara, I have created,
caused others to create, and rejoiced at the creation of negative karmas such as misusing
offerings to holy objects, misusing offerings to the Sangha, and stealing the possessions of
the Sangha of the ten directions; I have caused others to create these negative actions and
rejoiced at their creation.

I have created the five actions of immediate retribution, caused others to create them, and rejoiced at their creation. I have committed the ten nonvirtuous actions, involved others in them, and rejoiced at their involvement.

Being obscured by all this karma, I have created the cause for myself and other sentient beings to be reborn in the hells, as animals, as pretas [those living in the preta realm, one of the lower realms of existence], in irreligious places, among barbarians, as long-life gods, with imperfect senses, holding wrong views, and being displeased with the presence of a Buddha.

Now before these Buddhas, transcendent destroyers who are transcendental wisdom, who are compassionate eyes, who are witnesses, who are valid and see with their omniscient minds, I am confessing and accepting all these actions as negative. I will not conceal or hide them, and from now on, I will refrain from committing these negative actions again.

Buddhas and transcendent destroyers, please give me your attention. In this life and throughout beginningless lives in all the realms of samsara, whatever roots of virtue I have created through even the smallest acts of charity, such as giving one mouthful of food to being born as an animal, whatever roots of virtue I have created by guarding morality, whatever roots of virtue I have created by abiding in pure conduct, whatever roots of virtue I have created by fully ripening sentient beings' minds, whatever roots of virtue I have created by generating bodhichitta, whatever roots of virtue I have created of the highest transcendent wisdom.

Bringing together all these merits of both myself and others, I now dedicate them to the highest of which there is no higher, to that even above the highest, to the higher of the high, to the superior of the superior. Thus I dedicate them completely to the highest, fully

accomplished Enlightenment. Just as the Buddhas and transcendent destroyers of the past have dedicated, just as the Buddhas and transcendent destroyers of the future will dedicate, and just as the Buddhas and transcendent destroyers of the present are dedicating, in the same way I make this dedication.

I confess all my negative actions separately and rejoice in all merits. I implore the Buddhas to grant my request that I may realize the ultimate, sublime, highest transcendental wisdom. To the sublime conquerors, the best of human beings living now, to those of the past, and to those who have yet to appear, to all those whose knowledge is as vast as the infinite ocean, with my hands folded in respect, I go for refuge.

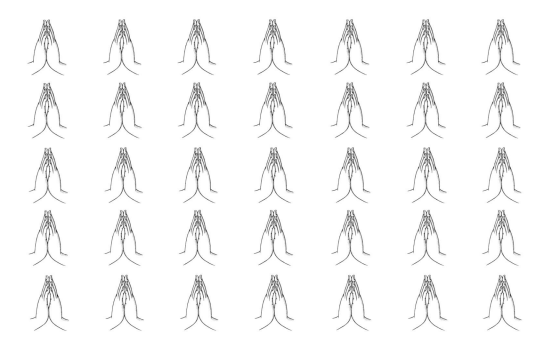

mantras and mudras

Mantras for removing obstacles

Here is a wonderful extract on the practice of chanting mantras, which I found from the archives of Lama Thubten Yeshe's teachings. Lama Yeshe was Rinpoche's guru, and he has reincarnated as Lama Osel Rinpoche who now studies at Sera Monastery in Southern India.

"There are two ways to recite mantras – verbal recitation and mental recitation. Mental recitation is more difficult because it involves the consciousness, whereas verbal recitation is much easier. Verbal recitation and mental recitation each have two ways; one is to concentrate on the seed syllable [the main syllable of a Buddha mantra] and mantra in written form, and the second is to concentrate just on the sound of the mantra.

"Lord Buddha's sutras are mantras. There is some force, an energy beyond the words themselves; [in this way,] so your speech becomes mantra. Mantras are more powerful than nuclear energy. The power of matter, the power of mantra, and the power of consciousness are the three powerful energies of the universe. Nuclear power is limited physical energy; mantra speech is more powerful; and consciousness is the most powerful.

"It is an incredible experience to recite mantras, the power is almost like magic. You can experience powers of mental telepathy, you can see all universal energy in front of you as if you are watching television. Sometimes you do not know what it is, you see an incredible reality."

THE MANTRA OF THE BEAUTIFUL GREEN TARA

One of the most popular mantras chanted by Buddhists to remove the disturbing obstacles of daily life is the mantra of the beautiful Green Tara, the female Buddha who is believed to have been born from the tears of compassion shed by the Compassionate Buddha:

OM TARE TUTTARE TURE SVAHA

Chant one mala (108 rounds) of this mantra each day. Chant it whenever you feel down and depressed, and develop a powerful imprint in your consciousness. Who knows then what may unfold for you? You can sing to this mantra; visualize beautiful Green Tara as you sing!

PRAISES TO THE 21 TARAS

The Praises to the 21 Taras is a very popular practice in Tibet (whether devotees have received initiation or not). This is because Tara is a very beloved Goddess among Tibetan Buddhists. The Praises to the 21 Taras is an extremely powerful practice.

Recited with faith, the the 21 Praises is a powerful prayer for removing obstacles, for gaining realizations, for success in business, and for curing illness.

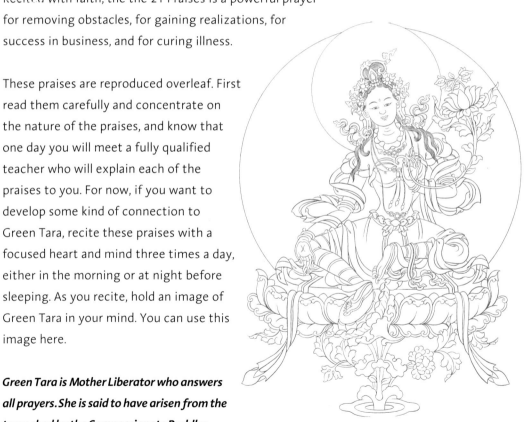

These praises are reproduced overleaf. First read them carefully and concentrate on the nature of the praises, and know that one day you will meet a fully qualified teacher who will explain each of the praises to you. For now, if you want to develop some kind of connection to Green Tara, recite these praises with a focused heart and mind three times a day, either in the morning or at night before sleeping. As you recite, hold an image of Green Tara in your mind. You can use this image here.

Green Tara is Mother Liberator who answers all prayers. She is said to have arisen from the tears shed by the Compassionate Buddha.

Let me and all who need protection
Enter beneath your right-hand mudra
Of granting boons and left-hand refuge mudra
And be relieved from every fear.

OM I prostrate to the noble transcendent liberator.

1.   Homage! Tara, swift, heroic!
       Eyes like lightning instantaneous!
       Sprung from op'ning stamens of the
       Lord of Three Worlds' tear-born lotus!

2.   Homage! She whose face combines a
       Hundred autumn moons at fullest!
       Blazing with light rays resplendent
       As a thousand-star collection!

3.   Homage! Golden-blue one, lotus,
       Water-born, in hand adorned!
       Giving, effort, calm, austerities,
       Patience, meditation, her sphere!

4.   Homage! Crown of tathagatas,
       Actions triumph without limit!
       Relied on by conqueror's children,
       Having reached ev'ry perfection!

5. Homage! Filling with TUTTARE,
    HUM, desire, direction, and space!
    Trampling with her feet the seven worlds,
    Able to draw forth all beings!

6. Homage! Worshipped by the all-lords,
    Shakra, Agni, Brahma, Marut!
    Honored by the hosts of spirits,
    Corpse-raisers, gandharvas, yakshas!

7. Homage! with Her TRAD and PHAT sounds
    Destroying foes' magic diagrams!
    Her feet pressing, left out, right in,
    Blazing in a raging fire-blaze!

8. Homage! TURE, very dreadful!
    Destroyer of Mara's champion(s)!
    She with frowning lotus visage
    Who is slayer of all enemies!

9. Homage! At the heart her fingers,
    Adorn her with Three Jewel mudra!
    Light-ray masses all excited!
    All directions' wheels adorn her!

10. Homage! She so joyous, radiant,
    Crown emitting garlands of light!
    Mirthful laughing with TUTTARE,
    Subjugating maras, devas!

11. Homage! She able to summon
    All earth-guardians' assembly!
    Shaking, frowning with her HUM sign
    Saving from every misfortune!

12. Homage! Crown adorned with crescent
    Moon, all ornaments most shining!
    Amitabha in her hair-knot
    Sending out much light eternal!

13. Homage! She 'mid wreath ablaze like
    Eon-ending fire abiding!
    Right stretched, left bent, joy surrounds you
    Troops of enemies destroying!

14. Homage! She who strikes the ground with
    Her palm, and with her foot beats it!
    Scowling, with the letter HUM the
    Seven levels she does conquer!

15. Homage! Happy, virtuous, peaceful!
    She whose field is peace, nirvana!
    She endowed with OM and SVAHA,
    Destroyer of the great evil!

16. Homage! She with joy surrounded
    Tearing foes' bodies asunder,
    Frees with HUM and knowledge mantra,
    Arrangement of the ten letters!

17. Homage! TURE! With seed letter
    Of the shape of syllable HUM!
    By foot stamping shakes the three worlds,
    Meru, Mandara, and Vindhya!

18. Homage! Holding in her hand the
    Deer-marked moon of deva-lake form!
    With twice-spoken TARA and PHAT,
    Totally dispelling poison!

19. Homage! She whom gods and their kings,
    And the kinnaras do honor!
    Armored in all joyful splendor,
    She dispels bad dreams and conflicts!

20. Homage! She whose two eyes bright with
    Radiance of sun and full moon!
    With twice HARA and TUTTARE
    She dispels severe contagion!

21. Homage! Full of liberating
    Pow'r by the set of three natures!
    Destroys hosts of spirits, yakshas,
    And raised corpses! Supreme! TURE!

    These praises with the root mantras
    And prostrations thus are 21!

From the prayer expressing the benefits of reciting the Praises to the 21 Taras:

    Who recites it wise and pious
    Full of faith towards the Goddess

    Quickly she'll be consecrated
    By seven times ten million conquerors.
    Gaining greatness herein, she will
    Reach at last the rank of Buddha.

    One who wants a child will get one,
    One desiring wealth will find wealth,
    One obtains all one's desires; by
    Hindrances one's not frustrated.

68 *mantras and mudras*

These Praises can be recited in rhythm. Do three rounds each day. Do not forget to precede your recitation of the Praises with the preliminary practices covered earlier, and do not forget to make dedications at the end. It is advisable to recite at least one mala (108 times) of the OM TARE TUTTARE TURE SVAHA before beginning the Praises.

One depends on the 21 aspects of Tara, with various actions that guide sentient beings … for example, those with shortage of life, in order to grant long life she manifests as White Tara. White Tara is not only for long life, she is also for wisdom. In former times, many enlightened ones developed wisdom with Tara. For those people who have small capacity or control, in order to grant the realizations of controlling, Tara manifests as Kurukulla. For those who have small wisdom, in order to develop wisdom, she manifests as Sarasvati. For those who cannot be subdued by peaceful means, she manifests as the protector, Palden Lhamo. Like this, there are 108 different female aspects, deities. All these are manifestations of Tara.

KYABJE LAMA ZOPA RINPOCHE

Mantras for making food offerings

Visualize the food on your dining table as wisdom nectar inside a vast, bejeweled container and offer this to Buddha visualized in your heart. Say OM AH HUM three times to consecrate the food, and then offer it with any or a combination of the following Food Offering mantras.

LAMA SANG GYAY LAMA CHO
DE ZHIN LAMA GAY DUN TAY
KUN GYI JAY PO LAMA TAY
LAMA NAMLA CHO PA BUL

TRANSLATION:
The guru is Buddha, the guru is Dharma
The guru is Sangha also
The guru is the source of all goodness and happiness
To all gurus I make offerings.

Let me share the food offering prayer (opposite) which I use in my own home. It was kindly given to me by a nun who helped me to complete a one-week Green Tara retreat in Aptos, USA. There is something magical about this food offering prayer; it really makes you tune into yourself very successfully so that the act of eating becomes a spiritual practice.

Recite the following:

 EH MA HO! *Food, drink, five meats, five nectars, all is in the skull*
Is in the nature of bliss and voidness
Purified, actualized, increased by the three Vajras
Becomes oceans of uncontaminated nectar.

OM AH HUM HA HO HRIH (say three times)

All faults of color, smell, taste, and potency are purified
The substances change into nectar.
It increases into an ocean and becomes blessed.

OM AH HUM (say three times)

Visualize: the nectar you are about to eat and all water, light, flowers, incense, and food offerings. Then say the multiplying mantra three times:

OM NAMO BHAGAVATE
VAJRA SARA PRAMARDANE TATHAGATAYA
ARHATE SAMYAKSAM BUDDHAYA
TA YA THA
OM VAJRE VAJRE
MAHA VAJRE
MAHA TEJA VAJRE
MAHA VIDYA VAJRE
MAHA BODHICHITTA VAJRE
MAHA BODHI MANDO PASAM KRAMANA VAJRE
SARVA KARMA AVARANA VISHO DHANA VAJRE SVAHA

Think: numberless Buddhas receive numberless offerings and generate great bliss. Then with hands in the mudra of prostration, offer to all direct gurus in the Lama Chopa merit field [visualize this lineage of gurus in the sky]; prostrate and make offerings to all the ten direction Buddhas and to all the statues, Stupas, scriptures, and thangkas throughout the worlds. All these are in essence the root (one's main) guru. They are empty from their own side. Generate great bliss!

Finally: offer to all beings in the six realms; think that they are liberated and attain Enlightenment.

Ho! At the dharmachakra center of the heart
Indestructible subtle wind and mind
Inseparable with supreme merit field
Gurus' assemblies, mind-sealed deities
To you we offer desire enjoyments
Of this circle of magnificent tsog.
Please take by being pleased and satisfied
In a state of uncontaminated bliss
Grant us the holy body, speech, and mind.
Please grant blessings to achieve in this life
Mahamudra profound vajra yoga
Inseparable with method and wisdom.

With every mouthful, continue the yoga of eating and drinking with this meditation.

With each drink and bite of food, offer it to yourself as the guru deity. In this way, one collects merit far greater than if you had offered this to all the numberless past, present, and future Buddhas, Dharma, and Sangha and all the ten directions' holy objects, statues, scriptures and Stupas. With the practice of this yoga, the food does not become pollution to your mind, a poison to be born in the lower realms, or a cause to block realizations. Eating only becomes great purification and collects most extensive merit; so each time it brings you closer to Enlightenment and makes your life more beneficial.

EIGHT OFFERINGS TO BUDDHA PRACTICED WITH MANTRAS AND MUDRAS

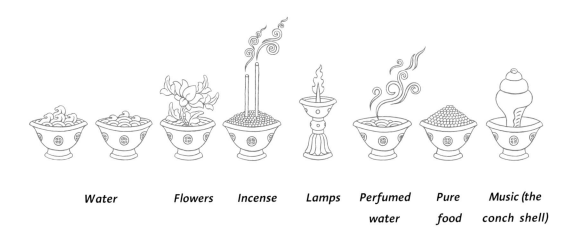

| Water | Flowers | Incense | Lamps | Perfumed water | Pure food | Music (the conch shell) |

The eight offerings to Buddha are water for drinking, water for washing the feet, flowers, incense, lamps, perfumed water, pure food, and music. Each of these eight offerings has its accompanying mudra and mantra. For those of you who may be interested in this wonderfully inspiring spiritual ritual, here is how you perform it.

Each offering is made with both a mudra (hand gesture), and the recitation of the mantra. Chant the mantra of the offering as you make the mudra with your hands.

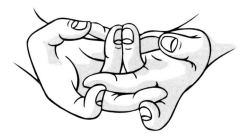

Offering hand mudra

For the mudras: first, one crosses the left wrist over the right in front of the breast, with the palms of both hands facing outward. Then gently snap the fingers simultaneously. This sends out the offering to goddesses who are carrying the offerings out from your heart. Then make a graceful turning gesture with your hands that culminates in the individual mudras that symbolize each offering substance (see below). This signifies the actual offering. Then, cross your right wrist in front of your left, with your palms facing inward toward your chest. Your right palm should be roughly facing your left shoulder and your left palm, your right shoulder. Again, snap your fingers gently. This brings the offering goddesses back into your heart.

1. Water for drinking:

OM ARGHAM AH HUM

The hands are held out at breast level to form the likeness of a shallow bowl. The little fingers and ring fingers are inside the bowl, the middle fingers are extended straight outward, and the index fingers are bent to touch the third joint of the middle fingers. The thumbs rest on the side of the hands. Chant the mantra as you make the hand gesture.

2. Water for washing the feet:

OM PADYAM AH HUM

With the left hand in a fist, palm upward, rotate the right hand gracefully from the palm down with fingers closed to palm upward, gradually unraveling the fingers like water flowing from the hand.

3. Flowers:

OM PUPE AH HUM

Interlace the fingers with hands held back-to-back at breast level, with the fingertips pointing upward. The tips of the index fingers touch, and the thumbs rest on the side of the index fingers.

4. Incense:

OM DHUPE AH HUM

Interlace the fingers with palms facing, index fingers extended parallel, and thumbs extended upward, like incense rising.

5. Lamps:

OM ALOKE AH HUM

With hands held out and the palms upward, curl all fingers into a fist, except the middle fingers, which are extended straight outward. The thumbs touch the middle joint of the middle fingers.

6. Perfumed water:

OM GANDHE AH HUM

With the left hand in a fist, palm upward, hold the right hand vertically, palm outward, thumb slightly curved, with the right wrist resting gently on the edge of the left hand.

7. Pure food:

OM NIUDE AH HUM

The hands gently form an open bowl with the thumbs slightly curled inward and the index fingers bent, to suggest a shallow blow containing food.

8. Music:

OM SHABDA AH HUM

The thumbs of both hands hold down the ring and little fingers while the index and third fingers of each hand are extended. Shake the fingers alternately as if playing a drum.

The above offering ritual is usually performed as part of holy pujas (devotional rituals) and as advanced practices. This visualization ritual is extremely powerful and, by performing the mudras and mantras correctly, one is said to have performed offerings of a vast cosmic dimension. If you wish, you can make these offerings on your altar in the form of eight beautiful bowls of pure, clear water. Or alternatively, to signify music, you can place a conch shell at the end of a row of seven water bowls.

How can the performance of rituals such as these aid in the expansion of wisdom? Buddhist masters have explained it to me thus. Neither the Buddhas nor the Bodhisattvas are in need of the offerings. Indeed, the elaborate hand gestures and mantras are nothing more than a means of generating a spirit of reverence and devotion.

They are also excellent preliminaries to developing stillness of mind and purity of concentration – both of which are worthwhile aids to preparing the mind to gain greater insights into the wisdom that comes with understanding the true nature of reality. So the more focused the mental visualization is, the more focused will be the concentration of making offerings. Eventually with practice one should be able to "see" jeweled bowls and fresh lotus flowers and one should be able to "see" the beautiful maidens in attendance wearing silk garments studded with jewels.

It is from the Buddhist practices of visualization that the secret magic of mental imaging has become available to the world.

THE EIGHT AUSPICIOUS OBJECTS

These absolutely auspicious offerings can be placed on altars, or anywhere around the home.

The parasol

The conch shell

The vase

The banner

The double fish

The mystic knot

The lotus

The wheel

The eight auspicious objects comprise of the parasol, the conch shell, the vase, the banner, the double fish, the mystic knot, the lotus, and the wheel.

MAKING OFFERINGS WITH HAND MUDRAS

It is possible to make different types of offerings in your meditative sessions by using a combination of mantras and mudras. Here are the mantras and mudras that symbolize the offering of the eight auspicious objects. Do this while seated in meditation at your altar or in a quiet place. Always begin by settling the mind so it becomes calm, taking a relaxed posture and then generating your motivation for doing this practice (see page 9).

You can make the offerings in any order you wish, but as you recite the mantra and make the hand mudra, visualize that these auspicious objects are being carried by eight Offering goddesses who emanate directly from your heart. If you have an image of a Buddha on your altar it will be even easier to visualize making these offerings.

1. Offering the mystic knot
May all beings always have good fortune by my offering this auspicious object of good fortune that is brought by this beautiful maiden, who is as fair as the moon's glow, proudly bearing aloft the glorious mystical coiled knot.

2. Offering the golden wheel
May all beings always have good fortune by my offering this auspicious object of good fortune that is brought by this beautiful maiden, who glows like jasmine, proudly, gracefully carrying the golden wheel.

3. Offering the lotus flower

May all beings always have good fortune by my offering this auspicious object of good fortune that is brought by this youthful and pure maiden, blazing with azure-blue light, bearing aloft the precious 100-petalled lotus flower.

4. Offering the banner of victory

May all beings always have good fortune by my offering this auspicious object of good fortune that is brought by this victorious green maiden, so skillful in the arts of amorous melody, singing sweetly as she raises the banner of victory.

5. Offering the white parasol

May all beings always have good fortune by my offering this auspicious object of good fortune that is brought by this bright-eyed maiden, who is the color of powdered vermillion, glancing coquettishly as she twirls the white pearl umbrella.

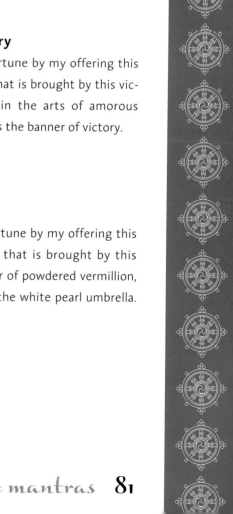

6. Offering the vase of treasure

May all beings always have good fortune by my offering this auspicious object of good fortune that is brought by this shapely maiden, white as the clouds on the horizon, enticingly holding a vase filled with treasures in her two hands.

7. Offering the right-turning conch shell

May all beings always have good fortune by my offering this auspicious object of good fortune that is brought by this glorious maiden, who is the color of stainless emerald, seductively carrying the right turning conch shell.

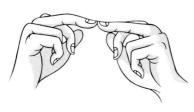

8. Offering the golden double fish

May all beings always have good fortune by my offering this auspicious object of good fortune that is brought by this ravishingly beautiful maiden, pleasing as a peacock, her eyes flashing like lightning as she holds the golden double fish.

food for thought

AN EXTRACT FROM LAMA YESHE'S TEACHINGS

" Charity is not an external giving; charity is inside.

A charitable attitude is the solution to an uptight,

miserly heart … you can do as much as you want

to with a good heart. For example, as a child I

remember my mother and father fighting. It

started when some poor people came to our

house; and these beggars kept coming, day in, day

out. Being practical, my mother wanted to give

them as much as she could. But my father said

that this was stupid, as the beggars were just lazy

and had an easy life, so why should she give to

those who took no responsibility? After all, we had

a hard-working life. My mother disagreed, saying,

"you can't do that," and continued to give to the

beggars from time to time. Yet my father, also

being practical, has a point; he wanted to give to

hard-working monks and nuns at the monasteries.

It was a small fight, but I don't know who was

right, and who was wrong."

Mantras for healing

There are seven Medicine Buddhas who manifest to overcome the health and death obstacles of all living beings. The Practice of the Medicine Buddhas is very powerful, not only for healing diseases, but for purifying the negative karma of those who recover from illness and those who succumb to it. This practice is also powerful for bringing success, temporary as well as ultimate.

When someone is seriously ill, Buddhists familiar with this practice usually do elaborate meditation and pujas (ritual offering ceremonies) addressed to each of the seven Medicine Buddhas. The effect of these pujas is always beneficial, whether the person recovers and lives, or yields to the illness and dies. They will recover immediately, or die within one or two days with a peaceful mind rather than in pain.

The Medicine Buddha practice is also performed to bring general success. Those who pray to the Medicine Buddha with a sincere and powerfully focused mind are said to be able to gain clairvoyance. A sign of attainment is that patients come to you in your dreams and you diagnose their illness; and the next day they actually do come to see you and you are able to prescribe the exact treatment they need. Another sign is that when you concentrate on the patient's pulse, you can immediately recognize the disease and prescribe the correct treatment. Also, as you are examining the pulse, many goddesses may appear floating around you, and reveal the nature of the disease and its treatment.

By reciting the Medicine Buddha mantra as a daily practice, all the Buddhas and Bodhisattvas will pay attention to us, just as a mother pays attention to her beloved child, and always guide us. This purifies all our negative karmas and quickly pacifies diseases and spirit harms. It also brings success; everything succeeds exactly according to our wishes.

Here is the short mantra of the Medicine Buddha:

TADYATHA
OM BHEKHANDZYE BHEKHANDZYE MAHA BHEKHANDZYE
RADZA SAMUDGATE SVAHA

The Medicine Buddha has a deep royal blue-colored body surrounded by a halo of rainbow light. His right hand is in the mudra of giving sublime realizations; in his lap, his left hand is in the mudra of concentration, holding a bowl that is filled with healing nectar.

Bhekhandzye means eliminating pain; *maha bhekhandzye* means the great elimination of pain.

One explanation of the meaning of the first *bhekhandzye* is that it refers to eliminating the pain of true suffering, not just of disease, but of all problems. It takes away the pain of death and rebirth that is caused by karma and disturbing thoughts. The first *bhekhandzye* eliminates all the problems of body and mind, including problems related to old age and sickness.

The second *bhekhandzye* in the mantra eliminates the true cause of suffering, which is not external but within the mind. This refers to karma and disturbing thoughts. It is the inner cause that enables external factors, such as food and exposure to sunlight, to become conditions for disease.

HOW TO USE THE MANTRA AT THE TIME OF DEATH

It is excellent, with a bodhichitta motivation, to recite the Medicine Buddha's holy name and mantra in the ear of a dying person or animal, because it will prevent their rebirth in the lower realms. If the dying person can no longer hear the mantras, you can recite them and then blow on their body. You can also apply perfume or talcum powder to the body, and then recite and blow in the same way.

HOW TO USE THE MANTRA TO INCREASE THE POWER OF MEDICINE

Tibetan doctors use Medicine Buddha mantras to bless their medicine with spiritual power, thereby bringing about a quick recovery and mental purification for their patients. By reciting this mantra, we too can increase the power of the medicine that we are taking or giving to others.

Place the medicine in a bowl in front of you and visualize a moon disc above it. Standing on the moon disc is a blue OM surrounded by the syllables of the Medicine Buddha mantra in a clockwise direction. As you recite the mantra, visualize nectar flowing down from every syllable into the medicine. The syllables dissolve into the medicine, which makes it very powerful. The more faith you have and the more mantras you recite, the more power the medicine will have. The efficacy of this practice depends on the intensity and purity of your own faith.

HOW TO USE THE MANTRA TO HELP THE SICK OR DYING

When you do the Medicine Buddha practice for a person who is sick or dying, recite the names of the seven Medicine Buddhas. Visualize them one on top of the other, above the person.

The names of the seven Medicine Buddhas are:

1. **Renowned Glorious King of Excellent Signs**
2. **King of Melodious Sound, Brilliant Radiance of Skill, Adorned with Jewels, Moon and Lotus**
3. **Stainless Excellent Gold, Great Jewel who Accomplishes All Conduct**
4. **Glorious Supreme One, Free from Sorrow**
5. **Melodious Ocean of Proclaimed Dharma**
6. **Clearly Knowing, by the Play of Supreme Wisdom of an Ocean of Dharma**
7. **Medicine Guru, King of Lapis Light**

Visualize that nectars are emitted from the first Buddha and purify the person of all negative karmas and obscurations. Recite the name of each Medicine Buddha seven times, in turn.

With the final Medicine Buddha, however, recite as many mantras as you wish and again visualize strong purification. Think that the person is completely purified; no negative karma at all exists in his or her mental consciousness, and the person's body becomes as calm and as clear as crystal.

The Medicine Buddha then melts into light and is absorbed within the person, blessing body, speech, and mind so that he or she becomes one with the Medicine Buddha. The person's mind is transformed into Medicine Buddha's holy mind. Meditate strongly on that oneness.

Mantras for multiplying the merits of meditation

MEDITATION

A successful meditation depends on your state of mind. Reciting certain prayers can induce the appropriate inner state. You can say prayers out loud or in your mind; what is vital is that you recite them with understanding and sincerity.

Chanting mantras is not the mechanical recitation of words. It is actually praying. It is an opening of the heart to communicate with our true nature. The words merely serve to remind us of what we are trying to achieve and they help us to create the cause of whatever we are praying for.

Mudra for meditation

One of the best ways to induce a wonderful preparatory state for spiritual meditation is to try to sit in a relaxed manner, and to position your hands in the Meditation mudra. Sit with a straight back and, if possible, in the Vajra position, which is the Buddha's lotus posture. Let the hands rest lightly on your lap in the mudra of meditation, which is shown here. Note that the right hand is resting lightly on the left hand.

The Meditation mudra.

I have discovered that one of best meditative mantras to chant is the mantra of the Heart sutra, also known as the mantra of the Perfection of Wisdom. It is wonderfully uplifting and intensely inspiring. This mantra is chanted in its original Sanskrit language. As you chant this mantra, visualize the Buddha Shakyamuni in the space in front of you, sending out light beams in all directions, blessing the world and filling the entire space around you with glorious white light. Here is the mantra:

TADYATHA OM, GATAY GATAY PARAGATAY
PARASAMGATAY BODHI SVAHA

Ten minutes of this meditation each morning will do wonders for your peace of mind. You will feel totally exhilarated and strengthened, ready for the day.

MULTIPLYING MANTRA

According to the sutras, if you recite this mantra seven times each morning, whatever virtuous actions one does that day, including the chanting of mantras, will be multiplied a hundred thousand times. So this is an excellent mantra to recite every morning to prepare you for the day's activities.

OM SAMBHARA SAMBHARA BIMANA SARA
MAHA DZAWA HUM
OM MARA MARA BIMANA KARA
MAHA DZAWA HUM

Mantras for empowerment

MANTRAS FOR BLESSING THE MALA

Buddhists have a rosary, which they call a mala. Malas are beads strung together and these can be made from precious stones, bodhi seeds, or any kind of material favored by you. Usually, a mala comprises 108 beads, so if you are asked to chant "one mala" of any mantra, it means to chant it 108 times. Malas also come in bracelet size, tied with either 21 or 28 beads. In recent years Buddha beads like these have become extremely popular, and even fashionable. Recite the Blessing mantra given on the following page seven times. Then, if you wish, blow onto your mala to enhance the power of subsequent mala-mantras.

OM RUTSIRA MANI PRAVARTAYA HUM

MANTRAS FOR BLESSING THE SPACE-ENHANCING BELL

Rinpoche so very kindly gave me this wonderful mantra for a special bell that I had designed for enhancing the chi (energy or life force) of the space around us. The bell is made from seven types of metal to symbolize the seven planets. The sound of the bell is extremely sweet and, due to the presence of the seven metals, it lingers and cleanses the space of all negative chi. Rinpoche advised me that I could chant this special mantra seven times on the bell as I ring it. This is a wonderful way of empowering the bell so that anyone hearing its sound would be purified of negative karma, and the space cleansed of all negative energy.

OM PEMO USHNISHA BIMALAY HUM PEY

OTHER EMPOWERMENT MANTRAS

For blessing the feet: when you recite this mantra three times and then spit on the soles of your feet, it will ensure that when you inadvertently step on and kill any creature, such as an ant, it will find rebirth in Pure Land.

OM KRAY TSA RAGANA HUM HRI SVAHA

For blessing any meat that you eat: when you recite this mantra seven times over any meat you eat, it purifies the fault of eating meat and it helps the animal whose flesh you are eating to be reborn in Pure Land.

OM AHBIRA KAY TSARA HUM

Mantras for longevity

Living life to a ripe old age is one of the most significant of life's blessings, simply because human life is deemed to be so extremely precious. Being born into the human realm is considered the most precious among rebirths in all the six realms of existence and this includes even the deva (or god) realms. And this is because Buddhists regard human rebirth as the one most conducive to the practice of Dharma – Buddha's teachings that show the unmistaken path to total liberation from karma, freedom from the endless round of birth and rebirth known as samsara.

So longevity is highly desirable, as is the clarity of mind to make our lives as meaningful as possible. The Buddha and Bodhisattva deities that make up the longevity trinity are White Tara, Amitayus, and Namgyalma and most Buddhist paintings on thangkas of these Buddhas will usually show the other two Buddhas on the bottom left- and right-hand corners. You can chant the mantras and do the practices dedicated to any one of these three Buddhas of longevity if you wish to pray for a long life either for yourself or, better still, for someone else.

WHITE TARA — THE GODDESS OF LONGEVITY

White Tara is one of the three longevity deities. White Tara has one face and three eyes on her face, and one eye on each palm of her hands and on each foot to make a total of seven eyes. The right hand rests across the knee in the mudra of Supreme Generosity. Her left hand holds the stem of a white lotus, which blossoms at her left ear. In a very peaceful mood, she is adorned with a tiara, a long and short necklace, gold and jeweled ornaments, and wears colored silk garments. Sitting in the Vajra posture above a moon disc and lotus seat, she is surrounded by colored rings and framed with pink lotus blossoms.

Visualize White Tara emanating white light, like beams of longevity, which enter into the body as you chant her mantra. Think strongly that the white light purifies you of all negative karma that may cause you untimely death. Think that you receive her longevity empowerments.

OM TARE TUTARE TUTTARE TURE MAMA AYUR
PUNYE JNYANA PUSHTIM KURU YE SVAHA

Dedicate the merit of this mantra recitation to your long life and the long life of all beings.

*The beautiful Goddess White
Tara is one of the deities who
grant the gift of longevity.*

THE MANTRA OF NAMGYALMA

This is a powerful mantra for purification and for longevity:

OM BHRUM SVAHA
OM AMRITA AYUR DA DAS SVAHA

Buddha Namgyalma

THE POWERFUL MANTRA AND PRACTICE OF BUDDHA AMITAYUS

Visualize the red Buddha Amitayus holding a long-life vase, with legs crossed in the Vajra position.

At the heart of Amitayus is a lotus and moon disc, and above that the seed-syllable HRIH. Visualize beams of red light emitting from HRIH in all directions, bringing into the vase all the essence of life in samsara, so it is filled with long-life nectar.

Next, visualize this nectar overflowing from the vase and entering the crown chakra of your head, flowing into all the psychic channels of your body so that you feel that your whole body and mind are embraced by this long-life nectar. The nectar completely purifies all your disease, spirit harms, negative karmas, and obscurations. These negatives flow out of your body completely. While doing this visualization, recite the mantra overleaf:

Buddha Amitayus is also one of the deities who bestow the gift of long life. His body is red in color and he holds the vase containing the nectar of long life.

NAMO RATNA TRA YAYA
OM NAMO BHAGAVATE
APARIMITA AYUR JNYANA
SUBINI SHITSA TATAYE
DZORA DZAYA
TATHAGATAYA
ARHATE SAMYAKSAM BUDDHAYA
TA YA THA
OM PUNYE PUNYE
MAHA PUNYE
APARIMITA PUNYE
AYU PUNYE
MAHA PUNYE
AYUR JNYANA
SARVA RUPA SIDDHI
AYUR JNYANA KAY TSE DHRUM
OM DHRUM
AH DHRUM
SO DHRUM
HA DHRUM
TSE DHRUM
OM SARVA SAMSKARA
PARISHUDDHA DHARMATAY
GAGANA SAMUDGATE
SVABHAVA BISHUDDHE
MAHA NAYA PARIVARA YE SVAHA

If you are pressed for time, you can recite the short mantra of Amitayus:

OM AMARANI JIVAN TIYE SVAHA

Benefits

The extensive merit of reciting this mantra just one time is inconceivable. It is the supreme protection from the eight aspects of death. Reciting this mantra stops all inauspicious signs, bad omens, and all black magic. One is able to eliminate hundreds of obstacles. Sickness can be removed, and all auspiciousness received.

The beneficial qualities of this mantra is beyond concept. Even the Buddhas and their princes, the Bodhisattvas, are unable to express the benefits of this mantra. The ultimate reality of it is the sound of itself. This completes the essence of all the Transcendent Inconceivable Life.

Mantras to the jambhalas – the wealth buddhas

The wealth Buddhas in the pantheon of Buddhist deities are known as Jambhalas, and there are several different Jambhala practices that are believed to be extremely powerful in relieving human beings of poverty and instead blessing them with wealth. Jambhala wealth rituals are best practiced with the motivation of supporting monasteries and financing charities, and the spread of Buddha's teachings.

There are basically three types of Jambhala practice: the making of wealth vases, making water offerings to Jambhalas, and reciting the mantras. These practices can be done to either one or all three different Jambhalas: the White Jambhala, who is seated on a dragon, the Yellow Jambhala, who is seated on a lotus, and the Black Jambhala, who is standing. All three Jambhalas hold a wish-fulfilling mongoose in their left hand, from whose mouth spills precious jewels and gemstones, which signify wealth given by Jambhalas.

THE WHITE JAMBHALA

Visualize this Jambhala filling your home with gemstones as you recite his mantra. Chant the mantra at least 108 times each day:

OM PADMA KRODA ARYA JAMBALA
HRI DAY A HUM PHET

The White Jambhala, one of three principal Buddhist wealth deities.

THE YELLOW JAMBHALA

The Yellow Jambhala sits with his right hand holding a fruit and his left hand holding a treasure-producing mongoose. Recite his mantra 108 times and make a strong wish for the Jambhala to bless you and your family with prosperity:

OM JAMBALA JALANDRAYE SVAHA

THE BLACK JAMBHALA

This Jambhala has a black body and is usually visualized with a wrathful face and standing surrounded by a ring of fire. Recite his mantra 21 times while making a strong prayer that wealth blessings are showered on you and your family:

OM INDRA-YANI MUKHAM BHRA-MARI SVAHA

Mantras for crying babies

NAMO MATI GANA JA TSE BUTE TSE SVAHA

Recite this mantra 100 times and blow on some water. Wash the baby's body with this water. Then mix this water with roasted flour to make a dough, and fashion from it a human shape. If the child cries in the night, put the figure above the front door. If the baby is crying at dawn time, put it below the door. If the child cries all night, put the figure under the mother's bed or under the blanket. If the child cries day and night, the mantra should be written on paper and kept around the child's neck. In this case it is advised that the mantra is written in Tibetan. It is best to try to get this from a high lama or from a geshe (qualified teacher).

Special Mantra Practices

How to practice a white light meditation

Relax and sit in whatever position you find comfortable, or lie down. The position of your body is not as important as the state of your mind when you meditate.

MOTIVATION

Always begin by generating a positive motivation. Ask yourself, "What is the purpose and meaning of my life? The purpose of my life is not just to solve my own problems and obtain happiness for myself. The purpose of my life is not small and narrow, but is as vast as the infinite space. It is my responsibility to free everyone from their problems and lead them to the ultimate happiness of full Enlightenment. To perform this extensive service for all beings, I must develop wisdom and method, and compassion for all beings. I must live a long life and have good health. For these reasons, I am doing this white light meditation."

MEDITATION

First breathe in slowly, and then breathe out. As you breathe out, visualize that all disease, spirit harms, unskillful actions, and thoughts inside you, and the imprints left by these on your consciousness, are purified. These bad things come out of your body as black smoke, and disappear into the earth.

Now, as you breathe in, visualize that strong light beams are emitted from the Stupas, which symbolize the perfect, pure mind of full Enlightenment. (Other objects of meditation can be used, such as Buddha images or other holy objects. If these do not feel comfortable to you, then draw upon other sources, such as crystals or universal healing energy.)

This white light illuminates your body, and lights you up inside, completely purifying you of all diseases, sprit harms, unskillful actions and thoughts, and the imprints left on your consciousness. Feel that your whole body is in the nature of white light. You have no more suffering and no more problems. Your mind and body are completely free of worry and negativities. From the top of your head down to your toes, your entire body is filled with great joy, with great, pure bliss.

After experiencing this great bliss, think that your life has been prolonged, and that your positive energy, the cause of your happiness and success, has been increased, as well as your understanding of the path to Enlightenment. Everything is fully developed within you.

Repeat this breathing meditation over and over again:

Breathe out and purify; breathe in and receive light and healing from the holy objects.

Feel that your whole body is in the nature of light, and filled with great joy.

DEDICATION

Now dedicate to all other living beings the positive energy you have collected through generating this positive attitude and performing this meditation.

"Due to all these positive actions, may I develop the ultimate good heart of pure altruism and achieve the peerless happiness of full Enlightenment. May I also lead everyone else to the complete peace of mind that is full Enlightenment. And due to all the merits of positive actions, may anyone who sees me, touches me, remembers me, talks about me, thinks about me, just by that action alone be freed immediately of all obstacles to happiness – disease, spirit harms, negative actions, obscurations – and quickly achieve the ultimate happiness of full Enlightenment."

Using the eleven powerful mantras

གྔ|ངྐ་ཀྵ་མེ་ཇ་ཀྵི་ཇ་ཀྱི་མཎྜ་ནྱི་ཇུཉ་དུསཤ་མུཏ་ད་སྔུ|| ༀ་ཧཱུྃ་སྔུཀྵའ་ཡ་སྔུ་ད་ཡུ་ཡུང་ནེ་སྔུཀྵ|ༀ་མཆི་པཥི་དྒཱ|ༀ་ཀ་ཀ་ནི་ཀ་ནི་རོ
ཙན་རོཙན་མེ་ཏུ་ནི་ཏུ་ནི་མི་ནུ་མི་ནེབ་ནི་ད་བྷ་ནི་ད་གབ་ནཀྵ་པ་རེ་བ་སྐྱེ་མེ་སྦ་སཏུ་ཙ་སྔུ|| ༀ་མ་ཆི་པཥི་ཧཱུྃ|
||ༀ་ཏུ་དྲུ་བ་ནྲ་རེ་ཡེ་སྔུ| ༀ་ཧྲཱུྃ་ཏུ་ར་ད་ས་བཛ་སཏ་སི་ཧྲི་པ་ལཿ |ༀ་ན་མོ་ཏ་གབ་ལེ་ས་ད་ནུ་ད་པ་རེ་ཧོ་ཧཱུྃ་ཧྲི་ཧྲུཿ
ཡད་ས་ག་ད་གཡཔཉ་ནེ་སྔུ་ཏྲུ་དྲུཾ་ཡཧྡ་སྔུ|ཧོ་ཧཱ་ཧཱ་ཧཱ་ཀྵོ་ནྱ་པུ་ཧཱི་ཧོ་ཧྲི་ཧུ་ཏྲི་ཏྲི་སབ་ཀ་མ་ཤུ་ལ་རེ་ཏི་ཧཱི་ཏུ་ནི
སྔུ|| ཧོ་པཏྲུཿ ཧྲི་ཀཿབ་ལི་ནུ་ཕ་དཔ| ༀ་མ་ཆི་པཥི་ཧཱུྃ| ||ན་མཿསབྦུ་རྙི་སོཉྒུཉ་དྒཀོ་ཊི་ནུན་པ་རེ་དྒཱ ན་སབ༠་ཞ
ཆི་ད་ནི་ཊྔུ་ཏུ་ནུ་ནན་སོ་ལ་ག་ལ་ཏེ་ཡཉི་དུ་ལ་ཡུ་ཧ|སྐད་སྱུ་ག་དུ་སྱུༀ་ན་ན་ཏུ་སྐུག་ཏུ་དུ་ཚྒླུ་ལུ་ཡ་བ་ཧོ་ཧྲི་སོ་ད
ར་སོ་ད་པསབ་ད་སྔུ་ག་ཏུ་ཊྔི་ན་བ་ལེ་ཞ་པུ་ཏེ་སོ་ཏུ་ཉ་ཡུ་སྟུ་ར་སུ་པསབ་ད་སྔུ་ག་ད་ས་མ་ཡཱ་བོ་ཀྵི་ཊུཟྔུ་དཥྱུྃ|
ཊུ་ཡཥོ་ཊུ་ཡཧམ་མ་སབ་པུ་ཕོ་ཉུ་ལ་རེ་ཏི་ ཉུཊྔི་ག་ཏུ་ཀ་ལྱིཆ་ར་སུ་དཥི་དྒཱི་ད་ད་ད་ར་སྱུ་ཊྔ|ༀ་སབ་ཏ་སྐུ་ག་ད
མ་ལ་ཧོ་ཊུ་ཉི་ནྱུ་རྱུ་བ་ལི་པུ་ཏེ་སོ་སྐྱ་དཔ་ཐ་ག་ཊུ་ཊུ་ཊུ་སེཉ་ར་ཊུ་ད་པ་སབ་ཀུ་ར་སཊུ་པསབ་ད་ཊྔ་ག་ཏུ་ཡཉི་བི་ཉ་ཟ
ཊེ་ཊུ་ཊེ་སྔུ| ༀ་ཏུ་དྲུ་བ་ནྲ་རེ་ཡེ་སྔུ||

The mantras included above have unbelievable power. Simply touching these mantras to the body of someone who has just passed away will ensure he or she does not get reborn in the hell realms. Placed above doorways into each room, anyone passing under them will be purified and blessed of all mental obscurations and pollutions.

1. Mantras of Chenrezig

Short mantra:

OM MANI PÄDME HUM

Long mantra:

NAMO RATNA TRAYAYA / NAMO ARYA NYANA SAGARA / VAIROCHANA BUHA RAJAYA / TATA-GATAYA / ARHATAY SAMYAKSAM BUDDHAYA / NAMO SARVA TATAGATA BYAY / ARHATAY BYAY / SAMYAKSAM BUDDHAY BYAY / NAMO ARYA AVALOKITESHVARAYA / BODHISATTVAYA / MAHA SATTVAYA / MAHA KARUNI KAYA / TAYATA / OM DARA DARA / DIRI DIRI / DURU DURU / ITAY VATAY / CHALAY CHALAY / PRACHALAY PRACHALAY / KUSUMAY KUSUMAY VARAY / ILI MILI CHITTI JALA APANAYAY SOHA

2. Medicine Buddha mantra (short)

TAYATA / OM BEKANDZAY BEKANDZAY MAHA BEKANDZAY [BEKANDZAY]** / RADZA SAMU-GATAY SOHA

3. Wish-Granting Wheel mantra

OM PEMO USHNISHA BIMALAY HUM PAY

4. Mantra of Buddha Mitrugpa

NAMO RATNA TRAYAYA / OM KAMKANI KAMKANI ROCHANI ROCHANI TROTANI TROTANI TRASANI TRASANI PRATIHANA PRATIHANA SARVA KARMA PARAM PARA NI MAY SARVA SATTVA NENCHA SOHA

5. Mantra of Kunrig (the deity who liberates from the lower realms)

OM NAMO BAGAVATAY / SARVA DURGATAY SHODHANI RAJAYA / TATAGATAYA / ARHATAY SAMYAKSAM BUDDHAYA / TAYATA / OM SHODHANI / SHODHANI / SARVA PAPAM BISHODHANI / SHUDAY BISHUDAY / SARVA KARMA AVARANA VISHODHANI SOHA

6. Stainless Beam mantra (1)

NAMA SAPTANAM SAMYAKSAM BUDDHA KOTINEN PARISHUDAY MA NA SI / ABYA CHITA PATISHTA TUNEN / NAMO BAGAVATAY / AMRITA AYU SHASYA / TATAGATASYA / OM SARVA TATAGATA SHUDI / AYUR BISHODHANI / SAMHARA SAMHARA / SARVA TATAGATA BIRYA BA LAY NA PRATI SAMHARA AYU SARA SARA / SARVA TATAGATA SAMAYA/ BODHI BODHI/ BUDDHA BUDDHYA / BODAYA / BODAYA / MAMA SARVA PAPAM AVARANA BISHUDAY / BIGATA MALAM / CHARA SU BUDDHYA BUDDHAY HURU HURU SOHA

7. Stainless Beam mantra (2)

NAMA NAWA NAWA TINAM / TATAGATA GAM GANAM DIWA LUKA NAMA / KOTINI YUTA SHATA SAHA SVANAM / OM BO BO RI / CHARI NI CHARI / MORI GORI CHALA WARI SOHA

8. Mantras of Namgyalma

Long mantra:

OM NAMO BAGAVATAY SARVA TRAILOKYA PRATIVISHISHTAYA / BUDDHAYA TAY NAMA / TAYATA / OM BHROOM BHROOM BHROOM SHODAYA SHODAYA / VISHODAYA VISHODAYA / ASAMA SAMANTA AVABASA SPARANA GATI GAGANA SOBHAVA VISHUDAY / ABHISHIN CHANTU MAM / SARVA TATAGATA SUGATA VARA VACHANA AMRITA ABHISHEKARA / MAHAMUDRA

MANTRA PADAI / AHARA AHARA / MAMA AYUS SAMDARANI / SHODAYA SHODAYA / VISHODAYA VISHODAYA / GAGANA SOBHAVA VISHUDAY / USHNISHA VIJAYA PARISHUDAY / SAHASRA RASMEE SANCHO DITAY / SARVA TATHAGATA AVALOKINEE / SHAT PARAMITA PARIPURANI / SARVA TATAGATA MATAY / DASHA BHOOMI PRATISH TITAY / SARVA TATAGATA HRIDAYA / ADHISH TANA ADHISH TITAY / MUDRAY MUDRAY MAHA MUDRAY / VAJRA KAYA SAMATANA PARISHUDAY / SARVA KARMA AVARANA VISHUDAY / PRATINEE VARTAYA MAMA AYUR / VISHU- DAY SARVA TATAGATA / SAMAYA ADHISH TANA ADHISH TITAY / OM MUNEE MUNEE MAHA MUNEE / VIMUNEE VIMUNEE MAHA VIMUNEE / MATI MATI MAHA MATI / MAMATI SUMATI TATATA / BHOOTA KOTI PARISHUDAY / VISPOOTA BUDDHAY SHUDAY / HEY HEY JAYA JAYA / VIJAYA VIJAYA / SMRARA SMRARA / SPARA SPARA / SPARAYA SPARAYA / SARVA BUDDHA ADHISH TANA ADHISH TITAY / SHUDAY SHUDAY / BUDDHAY BUDDHAY / VAJRAY VAJRAY MAHA VAJRAY / SUVAJRAY VAJRA GARBAY JAYA GARBAY / VIJAYA GARBAY / VAJRA JALA GARBAY / VAJROD BHAVAY / VAJRA SAMBHAVAY / VAJRE VAJRINI / VAJRAMA BAVATU MAMA SHARIRAM / SARVA SATTVA NENCHA KAYA PARISHUDDHIR BAVATU / MAY SADA SARVA GATI PARISHUDDHISH CHA / SARVA TATAGATASH CHA / MAM SAMASH VAS YANTU / BUDDHYA BUDDHYA / SIDDYA SIDDYA / BODHAYA BODHAYA / VIBODHAYA VIBODHAYA / MOCHAYA MOCHAYA / VIMOCHAYA VIMOCHAYA / SHODAYA SHODAYA / VISHODAYA VISHODAYA / SAMANTANA MOCHAYA MOCHAYA / SAMANTA RASMI PARISHUDAY / SARVA TATAGATA HRIDAYA / ADHISH TANA ADHISH TITAY / MUDRAY MUDRAY MAHA MUDRAY / MAHAMUDRA MANTRA PADAI SVAHA

Short mantra:

OM BHROOM SVAHA / OM AMRITA AYUR DA DAY SOHA

At the conclusion, recite:

OM AMITAY / AMITODA BHAVAY / AMITAY VIKRANTAY / AMITA GATRAY / AMITO GAMINI / AMITA AYUR DADAY / GAGANA KIRTI KARAY SARVA KLESHA KSHAYAM KARI YAY SOHA

9. Padmasambhava's mantra

OM AH HUM VAJRA GURU PEMA SIDDHI HUM

10. Milarepa's mantra

OM AH GURU HASA VAJRA SARVA SIDDHI PALA HUM

11. Mantras of Buddha Maitreya's promise

Mantra of Maitreya Buddha's promise

NAMO RATNA TRAYAYA / NAMO BAGAVATAY SHAKYAMUNIYAY / TATAGATAYA / ARHATAY SAMYAKSAM BUDDHAYA / TAYATA / OM AJITAY AJITAY APARAJITAY / AJITAN CHAYA HARA HARA METRI AVALOKITAY KARA KARA MAHA SAMAYA SIDDHI BARA BARA MAHA BODHI MENDA BIJA SMARA SMARA ASMA KAM SAMAYA BODHI BODHI MAHA BODHI SOHA

Heart mantra

OM MOHEE MOHEE MAHA MOHEE SOHA

Close heart mantra

OM MUNEE MUNEE SMARA SOHA

THE PRACTICE OF THE ELEVEN POWERFUL MANTRAS

Chanting the eleven powerful mantras creates inconceivable merits. It is truly the best when you are fortunate enough to receive them as oral transmissions from a high lama, and usually chanting them yourself actually creates the cause for just such an event to occur. There is no doubt in my mind at all that when you chant these or any of the other mantras in this little book with a good and sincere motivation in your heart, that you are certain to meet a perfectly qualified lama who will open your heart and transform your mind toward the pursuit of peerless happiness, the kind of happiness that comes from realizing the true nature of reality.

For beginners who are new to Sanskrit and may find the words difficult to pronounce, just read through the eleven powerful mantras in your mind. If you can, do it daily; if not, then perhaps once a week, chanting the mantras for three rounds. Then recall these benefits of chanting the eleven powerful mantras: Whatever person who merely touches, wears the mantras on one's neck like an amulet, hears, remembers, or talks about these mantras will never be reborn in the lower realms and will always be born in the midst of the supreme (Mahayana) vehicle by obtaining a superior form of rebirth. That person will also train perfectly in the three principal aspects of the path to Enlightenment. All beings who hear, see, touch, or talk about these mantras will be freed immediately from all types of obstacles and problems caused by harmful spirits.

USING THE MANTRAS AS AMULETS TO HELP A DEPARTING SOUL

It is very good to fold up written mantras, wrap them in blue cloth, and place these amulets around the neck of the dying or recently deceased person. However, they must be removed during any medical treatment, such as an injection, otherwise the amulets will obstruct the medication entering the person's body. You can also put the amulets on your altar and recite mantras to bless them before giving them to the dying person.

Mantras and the Inner Mind

A DELIGHTFUL AND PROFOUND EXPLANATION

The wonderful and dearly beloved Lama Yeshe, Rinpoche's guru and co-founder of the FPMT*, once answered questions about the recitation of mantras during the seventh meditation course he conducted at Kopan, Nepal, on December 2, 1974. I found Lama Yeshe's explanation so extremely beneficial. Reproduced here is a short extract.

"...Some people think reciting mantras is something external rather than something natural. Many people think that way. Reciting a mantra doesn't mean physically you're reciting it. Reciting a mantra, from my experience, is done without words, by listening to the inner sounds.

"This, the inner nature, the inner sound, has existed in your nervous system within your physical body since you were born. From taking an initiation, the sound – the mantra – is more integrated into one-pointedness [single focus]. Then you can more easily see your inner nature, rather than being completely distracted by external senses – or world object[s].

"Our schizophrenic mind cannot forget our emotional problems, can it? The memory and the bothering mind are always present. But when reciting a mantra, the wrong conceptions and the agitation in your mind are automatically purified. The mantra brings a sense of integration, rather than your mind being totally interrupted by a sense of attachment, a sense of gravitation. So mantras help integrate the mind and bring one-pointed contemplation.

* Foundation for the Preservation of the Mahayana Tradition

"Some think that reciting mantras distracts you from understanding emptiness (shunyata); that adhering to the mental discipline of a mantra distracts you from realizing shunyata. Yet is it the same thing? When you meditate on shunyata you still have time for eating, sleeping, talking, and drinking, so why not have time for mantras?

"Instead of listening to useless conversation, it's better to listen to the inner sounds.

"You cannot deny the existence of inner sound. Look at your breathing. Your nervous system movement has a natural sound, too, if you listen. A doctor listens at your chest when he's giving you a check-up; this is the sound of your brain and your nervous system moving. This inner sound is not something Mahayana Buddhists have made up. It is a scientific reality that exists within you. Even when babies cry they say "Ahhhhhhh!" Actually, before it comes from the mouth, the sound "ah" is already in his nervous system.

"All fundamental sounds, the universal sounds, good sounds and bad sounds, are all based on "ah"; without "ah", you cannot pronounce anything – bad or good."

Question "When you die, do you carry this inner sound within you?"

Lama "Yes, yes. Inner sound continues all the time. If there is energy, there is sound. All energy, all universal energy has sound. This is not a religious theory, this is a scientific discovery. So you intellectual people cannot deny this! I'm joking! It's true, isn't it? Within all energy there is sound."

Question "Why are mantras so much powerful when given to you by a guru?"

Lama "Maybe one reason is that the guru has good understanding and good experience. He doesn't freak out, you know – "Ah, you want mantras! I'll read one for you!" A real guru has practiced mantras, and he has certain kind of contemplation experience in retreat and has received the power of the mantra from his guru. Receiving a mantra is not like receiving an object.

"Mantras have been generated by Guru Shakyamuni up until now. So therefore, giving it to you is more powerful than you just taking it by yourself. The way the guru gives the mantra has power. The guru puts you into a certain situation that transcends the normal ordinary relative mind, and therefore can communicate with the sound vibration. So in this way, there is a particular communication when he gives a mantra, so the mantra becomes a transcendental mantra. Otherwise you just take words from a book, with an ordinary mind, and the mantra does not become transcendental.

Really, mantras have so much power. If you count a certain number of mantras with contemplation, it sort of instinctively opens your mind to perceive the realization of telepathic power, which is almost unbelievable.

"In Tibet, on many occasions mantras have been used as medicine. Monks can be doctors too, you know. For infection and pain in your nervous system, there are particular antidote mantras. Along with the mantras the doctors blow with their breath, you know, and they cure! It is healing; such powerful healing.

"Especially if someone becomes mentally disturbed, just counting mantras and putting on the rosary is automatically like putting ice in boiling water. The person soon becomes sooooo . . . peaceful.

"This is my experience. In the West you have injections, medicine, penicillin. In Tibet, they do mantras. Mantras cure. If you have a big sore and do a certain mantra, one blow can make it completely disappear! Do you think that's impossible?

"I remember one time that I had an infection [Lama shows a scar on his neck from a wound that was healed when he was a young boy.] My uncle did mantras and he blew the mantra to cure me. Once when he blew, all the infection inside the wound came out. Just one blow, you know. This was incredible. Now this is my own experience, but for you it may be difficult to believe. Anyway, you can find out for yourself; you don't necessarily need to take my word for it. Check it out and discover its truth. Mantras can heal.

"In the West, psychic healing nowadays has become very popular. When I visited Indiana, in the United States, a large group of people came; they were healers and they believed there is positive and negative spiritual energy within us. They asked me, 'Does this exist?' I told them yes, it does exist. People everywhere were extremely interested.

"Healing with mantras can heal wrong conceptions, and your agitated mind, like cooling hot boiling water. It can also cure physical problems. You can cure diseases. This is because mantras are energy, but not gross energy. They are supreme wisdom-power!

"Always, this energy is pure. It cannot be contaminated by an evil being. You cannot, can never, give bad vibrations to a mantra. You can get completely angry with a mantra, but mantras are pure within you. Material energy can be made impure, but mantra energy is always pure."

Three special ways to use mantras

Rinpoche, my precious guru, manifests his amazing kindness by teaching many of his students how to make the practice of Dharma amazingly easy. Rinpoche demonstrates clear understanding of the psyche of all of us. Many of us are simply so lazy and unfocused in our effort to transform the mind. Or we are too busy with our own lives. Not many of us have the time to sit and do long meditations.

So Rinpoche has taught us many wonderfully easy ways to practice. Let me share just three easy ways to practice Dharma and accumulate lots of merit, which is also enjoyable.

CIRCUMAMBULATING STUPAS

Rinpoche explained that there is enormous merit just circumambulating the Stupa while reciting mantras under your breath. It is for this reason that many Buddhists go on pilgrimage to places like Bodhgaya, the home of the Mahabodhi Stupa, or to Kathmandu, where the Bouddhanath Stupa is located. Circumambulating these holy Stupas creates powerful benefits and purification!

Stupas are the main holy objects of Buddhism, and according to the sutra teachings of Chenrezig (see page 34), the Compassionate-Eyed One :

"If a person circumambulates with devotion a Stupa or statue of Buddha, in his future lives his enemies will respect and surrender to him. He will become a person of quality, respected by and pleasing to other people. The temporal and ultimate benefits are infinite. Circumambulating is the supreme method to purify obscurations and close the door to the lower realms."

This text also adds,

"Any being who does one circumambulation of or one prostration to a Stupa is liberated completely from the karma to be born in any of the levels of hell. One becomes a nonreturner, and achieves highest Enlightenment."

From Kyabje Lama Zopa Rinpoche:

"Circumambulate an actual holy object or a visualized one while reciting this mantra [see opposite], which multiplies the number of prostrations or circumambulations one thousand times."

CHOM DEN DAY DE ZHIN SHEG PA DRA CHOM PA YANG DAG
PAR DZOG PAY SANG GYAY RIN
CHEN GYEL TSEN LA CHAG TSEL LO
NAMO BHAGAVATE RATNA KETU RADZA
TATHAGATAYA ARHATE SAMYAKSAM BUDDHAYA
TADYATHA
OM RATNA RATNE RATNE MAHA RATNE RATNA BIDZA YE SVAHA

The following mantra increases the merit of
circumambulation one thousand times:

NAMO DASHA DAKTI KALA SARVA RATNA
TARYA YA NAMA PARDAKHAY
SARVA PAPAM
BISHODHANI SVAHA

*Circling a Stupa while reciting mantras is a way
to be free of the karma that causes rebirth in the
lower realms of existence.*

HANGING PRAYER FLAGS

One of the easiest ways to use mantras to benefit all the living beings of the world is to hang prayer flags so that each time the wind blows and wafts against the mantras, they send blessing energy in all ten directions thereby purifying every living creature that they touch. The ten directions comprise the eight directions of the compass, and two more: above (heaven) and below (earth). The merit is thus infinite and so it brings blessings and a great deal of purification that dissolves all the obstacles in your life. Rinpoche happily encourages us to hang prayer flags in our homes as a form of Dharma practice.

When you hang prayer flags to bring success, it is a good idea to put them up on the correct days, otherwise if the astrological date is incorrect, the prayer flag will continuously bring obstacles rather than actualize positive things. And then for as long as the prayer flags last, obstacles continuously arise. This also applies to long prayer flags and to banners.

According to the Tibetan lunar calendar, the following dates for hanging prayer flags and banners are wrong:

10th and 22nd of the first, fifth, and ninth months
7th and 19th of the second, sixth, and tenth months
4th and 16th of the third, seventh, and eleventh months
1st and 13th of the fourth, eighth, and twelfth months

If you do not have access to a Tibetan lunar calendar, you may use a special practice known as Controlling the Elements (jungwa ur nang), and this controls the obstacles caused by engaging in activities on the wrong astrological dates. There are special mantras to overcome this affliction, and the mantra used depends on the direction in which the prayer flags are hung.

mantras and mudras

So when you hang prayer flags, irrespective of whether your dates are correct or incorrect, it is a good idea to chant the antidote mantras.

Hanging prayer flags is good Dharma practice. Flags or banners in the wind send out blessings to the ten directions.

ANTIDOTE MANTRAS AND RITUALS

There are mantras that can be used to overcome doing anything at a bad astrological time and date including the hanging of prayer flags. These mantras are excellent for overcoming similar afflictions for starting a journey, opening a shop, or building a house on a wrong time and date.

In the east, place a metal object there, such as a metal windchime, and then recite:

MAMA KARA KARA YE SVAHA

In the south, put water there and recite:

MAMA KAM KAM YE SVAHA

In the west, put fire there (such as lighted incense or a box of matches) and recite:

MAMA RAM RAM YE SVAHA

In the north, put some earth there (such as sand in an incense container) and recite:

MAMA SU SU YE SVAHA

In each corner place a bundle of various plants, and recite:

MAMA POTA POTA YE SVAHA

Recite also the Heart mantra of the Eight Appearances:

OM AGANI NIGANA ACHALA MANDALA MATAYA SVAHA

By reciting this, you will not receive all the shortcomings. This means that everything will be very auspicious, and you will receive great happiness and goodness.

This method can stop all obstacles and negativities that arise from starting activities related to living and dying at the wrong time — for example, starting a journey, getting married, erecting a building, or taking a deceased person out of the house. If you start these activities at the wrong time, you will encounter a lot of obstacles according to how bad that day was for starting the activity. Many details are given in Tibetan astrology.

In the case of marriage, there will be a lot of fighting and disharmony between the couple. Even if the couple continue to live together, many other obstacles can arise.

If you start the construction of a building at the wrong time, many inauspicious things and problems can occur during construction. When building, you should request permission from the landlord. This does not refer to the person who owns or sold you the land, but to the landlord naga — the spirit of the land.

Ask permission and dig at the right point so that you don't harm the landlord. This helps to bring about the success of the construction and health, long life, and harmony to the family or people living in the house, monastery, or nunnery.

If you start a journey at the wrong time, you will constantly face problems. By starting a journey at the right time, you can avoid car accidents or airplane crashes.

If you take a deceased person out of the house at the wrong time, you will be confronted by obstacles in life or suffer illness. Choosing the right date protects you from these afflictions.

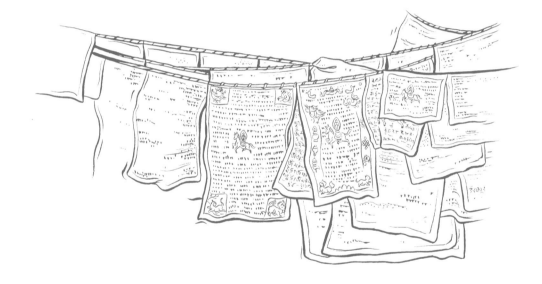

The benefits of prayer wheels

Prayer wheels are beautifully crafted holy objects that are filled with millions of the six-syllable OM MANI PADME HUM mantra, usually reduced to microfilm size to take advantage of modern technology.

A prayer wheel decorated with beautiful images of Offering goddesses.

One of the benefits of the prayer wheel is that it embodies all the actions of the Buddhas and Bodhisattvas of the ten directions. To benefit sentient beings, Buddhas and Bodhisattvas manifest in the prayer wheel to purify all our negative karma and cause us to actualize realizations on the path to Enlightenment.

All the beings (not only the people but also the insects) in the area where the prayer wheel is built are saved from rebirth in the lower realms. If you have a Mani prayer wheel in your house, your house is the same as the Potala, the Pure Land of the Compassionate Buddha. If you die next to a prayer wheel, the prayer wheel becomes the means by which your consciousness is transferred to a Pure Land. Simply thinking of a prayer wheel helps a dying person enjoy the karma that propels the consciousness up the central channel of the body and out through the crown chakra (energy center) to reincarnate in the Pure Land of Amitabha, or the Compassionate Buddha.

Simply touching a prayer wheel brings about a purification of negative karma. Turning a prayer wheel containing 100 million OM MANI PADME HUM mantras accumulates the same merit as having recited 100 million OM MANI PADME HUMs.

The prayer wheel at Land of Medicine Buddha, one of Rinpoche's meditation centers in California, US, contains 11.8 billion mantras, so turning it one time is the same as having recited that many mantras. So with such a giant prayer wheel, in just a few seconds one can perform so much powerful purification and accumulate so much merit. Turning the prayer wheel once is the same as having done many years of retreat.

There are earth, water, fire, and wind prayer wheels.

The water prayer wheel With the water prayer wheel, the water that touches the wheel becomes blessed. When that water goes into an ocean or lake, it carries the power to purify all the billions of animals and insects there. If you write the mantra on stones and then leave these stones near water that flows into ponds, the mantra written on the stone purifies all the water inside the pond. Such stones are named after the mantra inscribed upon them. The stone shown here is a Mani stone, which holds the mantra OM MANI PADME HUM.

A Mani stone is inscribed with a mantra, which purifies all the water touched by it.

The fire prayer wheel A fire prayer wheel is turned by the heat of either a candle or an electric light. The light that comes from the prayer wheel then purifies the negative karma of the living beings it touches.

The wind prayer wheel The wind that touches the prayer wheel is blessed by the power of the prayer wheel, which then has the power to purify the negative karma and obscurations of any being whom it touches.

PRAYER WHEELS USED IN HEALING

Rinpoche says that prayer wheels can be used for healing. Anyone with a disease such as AIDS or cancer, whether or not they have any understanding of Dharma, can use the prayer wheel for meditation and help in the healing process.

There are two prayer wheel visualizations. With the first, you visualize light beams coming from the mantras inside the prayer wheel, illuminating you and purifying you of all your disease and the causes of disease, your negative thoughts, and the imprints of these left on your mental continuum. You then visualize the light illuminating all sentient beings and purifying all their sufferings, as well as their negative karma and obscurations.

With the second visualization, you imagine beams emitting from the mantras and, like a vacuum sucking up dust, they collect all disease and spirit harms and, most importantly, the causes of disease, which are negative karma and obscurations. All these are absorbed into the prayer wheel.

If you are seriously ill, you can recite five or ten malas (108 rounds) of the OM MANI PADME HUM mantra and, as you recite, visualize yourself being purified of all karma that is causing you illness in this way.

At the end, again recite some more malas while visualizing that the beams emitted from the prayer wheel purify all the sufferings and obscurations of the sentient beings of the six realms. These absorb into the prayer wheel and all sentient beings, including you, are then liberated, actualizing the whole path and becoming the Compassionate Buddha. You can also practice circumambulations of the Stupa (see page 121) using the same visualizations.

It is thought that if someone with AIDS, cancer, or some other disease meditated like this and every day, for as many hours as possible, there would definitely be some positive effect.

Kyabje Lama Zopa Rinpoche says:

"I would like to emphasize that every large
and small prayer wheel
can be used by sick people for healing.
This practice is very
practical and very meaningful."

special mantra practices **133**

Making light offerings

It is said in the Ten Wheel Sutra:

All comfort, happiness, and peace in this world
come from making offerings to the Triple Gem –
the Buddha, the Dharma, and the Sangha.

Light offerings can be candles, electricity lights, or butter (oil) lamps. Before putting on the lights, generate your bodhichitta motivation (see page 9), and then think of a specific project for which you want blessings for success.

The hand mudra for the light offering of lamps.

Then as soon as you turn on the lights or light the candles, always say OM AH HUM three times. In general if you do not bless the offerings immediately by saying this three-syllable mantra, they can be usurped by wandering spirits and then the offerings become obstacles, rather than merit, for your practice. They will cause mental unrest by making you fall asleep while reciting your mantra, or by encouraging your mind to wander and become distracted. This advice should be followed for all types of offering.

A MANTRA TO INCREASE LIGHT OFFERINGS

Chant this beautiful mantra to increase the light offerings manifold. This same mantra can be used for all other offerings. Say the mantra three times:

OM NAMO BHAGAVATE VAJRA SARVA PRAMARDANAY,
TATHAGATAYA
ARHATE
SAMYAK SAM BUDDHAYA TADYATHA OM VAJRAY VAJRAY
MAHA VAJRAY
MAHA TEDZA VAJRAY
MAHA VIDYA VAJRAY
MAHA BODHICHITTA VAJRAY
MAHA BODHI MENDO PASAM
KRAMANA VAJRAY
SARVA KARMA AVARANA BISHO DANA
VAJRAY SVAHA

By the power of the truth of the Triple Gems, the blessings of all the Buddhas and Bodhisattvas, the great richness of having completed the two merits and the inconceivable pure sphere of existence, may all offerings become suchness.

THE VISUALIZATION

Visualize making the offerings to all the Buddhas and most of all, if you have a guru, make these offerings to your guru. In Tibetan Mahayana Buddhism, the guru is the most powerful object of devotion in the merit field [the visualized lineage of gurus and buddhas] and by making offerings to one's guru, the merit accumulated is beyond extensive! It is said in all the teachings of the Enlightened Ones:

"Abandon making other offerings; try purely to make offerings only to your guru. By pleasing your guru, you will achieve sublime wisdom of the omniscient mind."

In the root text *Buddhaya*, Guru Vajradhara said:

"The merit accumulated by making offerings to just one pore of the spiritual master is more sublime than that accumulated by making offerings to all the Buddhas and Bodhisattvas of the ten directions."

LIGHT OFFERING PRAYER

Say as many times as you wish:

I offer these clouds of actual and mentally created light offerings that in number equal the infinite sky – all manifestations of my own innate awareness, to all the gurus, to the Triple Gem and to all the Stupas, and holy objects which are all manifestations of my own root [main] guru.

DEDICATION

By the positive potential I have created by making this offering practice, may the bodhichitta mind in me not yet born arise and grow. May that born have no decline but increase forever more.

Due to this merit may the light rays of five wisdoms completely purify all my negative karma, and that of all those who have asked me to pray for them, all those who pray for me, all my friends and relatives, both living and dead, as well as all beings, living, transmigratory, and dead.

May all their sufferings cease right now

May all the three obstacles be immediately pacified now

May all their wishes for happiness be actualized immediately

May all impure appearances be purified

May they never be born in the lower realms

May they all have rebirth in the Pure Land of all the Buddhas.

Special mantras to increase merit 100,000 times

CHOM DEN DAY DE ZHIN SHEG PA
DRA CHOM PA YANG DAG PAR DZOG PAY SANG GYAY
NAM PAR NANG DZAY
O KYI GYELPO LA CHAG TSEL LO
(SAY THREE TIMES)

JANG CHUB SEMPA SEMPA CHENPO
KUNTU ZANG PO LA CHAG TSEL-LO
(SAY THREE TIMES)

TADYATHA OM PENTSA DRIYA AVA BODHI NAY SVAHA
(SAY SEVEN TIMES)

OM DURU DURU
DZAYA MUKHE SVAHA
(SAY SEVEN TIMES)

Mantras to make your wishes come true

Start with the preliminary prayer. Sit in a meditative pose, calm your mind and strongly concentrate on what you wish for, and then chant one mala (108) of these mantras each day. You can also copy them onto a piece of yellow paper and place them under your pillow when you sleep to empower your sleep with focused concentration. Visualize Shakyamuni Buddha sending out light rays in all the ten directions, and these rays entering your body through your crown chakra (energy center), thereby empowering you further.

DEZHIN SHEG PA TZA TZING
GYELPO LA CHAG TSEL LO
TADYATHA DARI DARI
DAR NE VAJRA SVAHA

This second mantra opposite is a special mantra to empower your prayers with greater strength so that what you pray for may come to pass. Recite this mantra three times after any of your meditative sadhanas.

CHOM DEN DAY, DE ZHIN SHEG PA,
DRA CHOMPA, YANG DAG PAR,
DZOG PAY SANG GYAY, NGO WA DANG,
MON LAM TAM CHAY, RAB TU DU PA
GYELPO LA, CHAG TSEL LO

Mantras can be recited any time, anywhere. It is not necessary to recite them out loud; let them stay at the edge of your mind. You may use a mala to count your mantras if you wish, or you can chant them subconsciously all through the day – while you bathe, while you work, while you eat, while you are walking, and even when you are sleeping. After a while, holy mantras will become a meaningful part of your life … and as your own inner wisdom-energy begins to surface, your life will become joyous and meaningful.

special mantra practices **141**

My motivation in creating this small book

Is that it creates the cause for happiness

For all sentient beings . . .

May all who read these mantras

Be free of sufferings and the causes of sufferings

Have only happiness and the causes of happiness

Abide in equanimity always

And never be separated from the bliss of high rebirth.

I dedicate whatever merit created

To the long life of my precious holy lama

Kyabje Lama Zopa Rinpoche

To whom I prostrate, make offerings, and take refuge.

May whoever reads this book

Create the cause for meeting

Perfectly qualified teachers

Just as I have.

LILLIAN TOO

NOTES

The translation of the Praises to the 21 Taras on pages 64–8 is based on Martin Wilson's chantable translation of the Praises to the 21 Taras. This version was additionally checked against the Tibetan and for euphony by the staff of the FPMT Education Department with the assistance of Ven. George Churinoff, January 2001.

The Food Offering Prayer on pages 70–3 is from Kirti Rinpoche, rendered into verse by Ven. Paula Munro.

Index